Cybersecurity

Protecting Your Shit in the Digital Wild West

Herkimer Throckmorton

ISBN: 9781779661708
Imprint: Telephasic Workshop
Copyright © 2024 Herkimer Throckmorton.
All Rights Reserved.

Contents

Introduction to Cybersecurity   1
The Importance of Cybersecurity in the Digital Age   1
The Evolution of Cybercrime   12
Ethical and Legal Considerations in Cybersecurity   26

Securing Your Fortress: Building Strong Defenses   43
Creating a Cybersecurity Mindset   43
Passwords: The Gatekeepers of Your Digital Shit   56
Protecting Your Devices and Networks   70
Social Engineering: Manipulating Human Sh*theads   84

The Wild West of Data: Privacy and Protection   97
Understanding Data Privacy   97
Safeguarding Your Online Identity   109
Encryption: Locking Sh*t Up   118
Cloud Security: The Digital Playground   127

Battling Cybercrime: Taking the Fight to the Wild West   139
Cybersecurity Careers: Riding Into the Sunset of Job Security   139
Collaboration and Cooperation in the Cybersecurity Community   152
The Future of Cybersecurity   163

Index   173

Introduction to Cybersecurity

The Importance of Cybersecurity in the Digital Age

Understanding the Growing Threats in the Cyber World

As we navigate the vast and treacherous landscape of the cyber world, it is essential to understand the various threats that lurk in the shadows. In this section, we will delve into the growing dangers of cyber-attacks and explore the techniques employed by cybercriminals to wreak havoc on unsuspecting individuals and organizations. So, strap in and get ready to learn what you're up against, because this shit is about to get real.

The Rise of Cybercriminals

In the past, hackers were often portrayed as loners in dark basements, wreaking havoc for the thrill of it. But today, cybercriminals have evolved into sophisticated and organized entities, motivated by both financial gain and political agendas.

One of the most prominent threats is posed by criminal organizations, who operate like a well-oiled machine. These enterprising individuals leverage advanced techniques, such as malware, ransomware, and botnets, to exploit vulnerabilities in systems and gain unauthorized access to sensitive information. Their primary objective is usually financial, whether through stealing credit card information, conducting identity theft, or extorting organizations for huge ransom payments.

Another rising threat comes from state-sponsored attacks. Nation-states engage in cyber warfare, aiming to gain a strategic advantage over their adversaries. These attacks can range from espionage and intelligence gathering to disruptive actions like unleashing destructive malware or compromising critical infrastructure. The stakes are high, and the consequences can be catastrophic.

The Weaponization of Technology

Technology has revolutionized the way we live, work, and communicate, but it has also become a weapon in the hands of cybercriminals. Let's take a look at some of the most common and dangerous threats in the cyber world.

    1. **Malware:** Malicious software, or malware, is the digital equivalent of a biological weapon. It includes viruses, worms, trojans, and ransomware that surreptitiously infiltrate systems, wreaking havoc once inside. Malware can cause data loss, financial damage, and even lead to the complete shutdown of critical infrastructure.

    2. **Phishing Attacks:** Phishing attacks are like fishing with a net made of deceit. Cybercriminals send fraudulent emails, pretending to be legitimate entities such as banks or government agencies, in an attempt to trick users into revealing sensitive information or downloading malicious attachments. These attacks have become increasingly sophisticated, making them difficult to spot.

    3. **DDoS Attacks:** Distributed Denial of Service (DDoS) attacks are the equivalent of a digital bombardment. By overwhelming a target system with a flood of traffic, cybercriminals can render it inaccessible to legitimate users. These attacks can disrupt websites, online services, and even cripple large-scale networks.

    4. **Social Engineering:** Cybercriminals are skilled manipulators who exploit human vulnerabilities to gain unauthorized access. Through techniques like pretexting, baiting, and tailgating, they trick individuals into revealing sensitive information or performing actions that compromise security. Remember, folks, trust is a precious commodity in the digital wild west.

Emerging Threats and Vulnerabilities

As technology leaps forward, new threats and vulnerabilities emerge on the horizon. Here are a few that deserve your attention:

    1. **Internet of Things (IoT) Vulnerabilities:** The proliferation of interconnected devices in our daily lives opens up a Pandora's box of security risks. From smart homes to wearable devices, each connected IoT device represents a potential entry point for cybercriminals to exploit, leading to privacy breaches, data theft, and even physical harm.

    2. **Cloud Security Concerns:** Cloud computing offers unparalleled convenience and scalability. However, it also introduces a host of security concerns. With sensitive data being stored and transmitted through remote servers, securing cloud-based resources becomes paramount. Failure to do so can result in data breaches and unauthorized access.

3. **Emerging Technologies:** As we embrace cutting-edge technologies like artificial intelligence (AI) and quantum computing, we need to be aware of the potential risks they bring. AI can be used maliciously to automate attacks and deceive users, while quantum computing poses new challenges to cryptographic systems, potentially rendering current encryption methods obsolete.

Protecting Yourself in the Cyber Wild West

Now that you have a glimpse into the cyber threats lurking in the shadows, it's time to arm yourself with the knowledge and tools you need to protect your digital shit. In the next sections, we will delve into the strategies, best practices, and precautions you can take to build strong defenses against these adversaries.

But remember, this is just the beginning of your journey. The cyber wild west is constantly evolving, and new threats will appear like cacti in the desert. So, stay alert, stay informed, and never stop learning, because your digital well-being depends on it.

Key Takeaways:

- Cybercriminals have become more organized and sophisticated in their attacks, with financial gain and political motives driving their actions.
- Malware, phishing attacks, DDoS attacks, and social engineering are some of the most prominent threats in the cyber world.
- Emerging threats include vulnerabilities in IoT devices, cloud security concerns, and the potential risks associated with emerging technologies like AI and quantum computing.
- The journey to cyber defense starts with awareness, knowledge, and continuous learning.

Now, grab your virtual cowboy hat and let's ride into the next chapter, where we'll learn how to build strong defenses to protect your digital shit in this wild and unforgiving frontier.

Real-Life Consequences of Cyber-Attacks

In the digital age, where our lives are increasingly intertwined with technology, the consequences of cyber-attacks can be devastating. It's not just about losing access to your favorite cat videos or compromising your embarrassing search history. Cyber-attacks can have far-reaching impacts on individuals, businesses, and even entire nations. In this section, we will explore the real-life consequences of cyber-attacks and understand why we need to give a shit about cybersecurity.

Financial Losses: Emptying Your Digital Piggy Bank

One of the most immediate and tangible consequences of a cyber-attack is financial loss. Cybercriminals are constantly on the prowl, looking for opportunities to steal your money or sensitive financial information. They employ various tactics such as phishing, ransomware, and identity theft to gain unauthorized access to your financial accounts.

Imagine waking up one morning to find all your bank and credit card accounts emptied. Your hard-earned money, savings, and investments gone in an instant. This is the harsh reality for thousands of individuals and businesses who fall victim to cyber-attacks every day.

Not only can cyber-attacks drain your accounts, but they can also result in unauthorized transactions, fraudulent purchases, and even the loss of your entire life savings. The financial burden and stress caused by such attacks can have a long-lasting impact on individuals and families, leading to bankruptcy, foreclosure, and shattered dreams.

Real-World Example: In 2014, retail giant Target suffered a massive data breach that exposed the personal and financial information of over 40 million customers. The cybercriminals behind the attack used malware to steal credit and debit card data, resulting in fraudulent transactions and unauthorized purchases. Target had to pay a hefty $18.5 million settlement to various financial institutions affected by the breach, not to mention the significant damage to their reputation.

Identity Theft: Becoming Someone Else's B*tch

Your personal information is a goldmine for cybercriminals. With just a few key details, they can assume your identity and wreak havoc on your life. Identity theft is one of the most common and devastating consequences of cyber-attacks. Once your personal information is compromised, cybercriminals can open new lines of credit, take out loans, and even commit crimes in your name, leaving you to deal with the fallout.

The effects of identity theft can be long-lasting and far-reaching. It can take years to fully recover from the financial, emotional, and psychological damage caused by identity theft. Victims often face the burden of proving their innocence, clearing fraudulent debts, and rebuilding their credit history. In some cases, victims have been wrongfully arrested or denied employment due to the actions of cybercriminals.

Real-World Example: In 2017, credit reporting agency Equifax suffered a massive data breach, exposing the personal information of over 147 million people. The stolen data included names, social security numbers, birth dates, and even credit card information. This breach led to a surge in identity theft cases, with victims struggling to protect their financial and personal lives.

Reputation Damage: Love, Sex, and Cyber-Shame

In today's connected world, our digital footprint plays a significant role in shaping our personal and professional lives. A single cyber-attack can tarnish your reputation and have long-lasting consequences.

Imagine waking up to find that your intimate and private photos have been leaked online for the world to see. This is the reality for countless individuals who have fallen victim to revenge porn attacks or unauthorized disclosure of sensitive information. The psychological and emotional toll of having your private moments exposed can be devastating, leading to depression, anxiety, and even suicide.

Beyond personal attacks, businesses and organizations also face the risk of reputation damage due to cyber-attacks. Data breaches that expose customer information can erode trust and loyalty, leading to a loss of customers, revenue, and ultimately, the downfall of the organization.

Real-World Example: In 2015, Ashley Madison, a dating website for married individuals seeking extramarital affairs, suffered a massive data breach. The personal information of over 32 million users was leaked online, exposing individuals' private desires and compromising their relationships. The fallout from the breach led to divorces, resignations, suicides, and a significant blow to the company's reputation.

Critical Infrastructure Disruption: Lights Out, No More Netflix

Cyber-attacks are not limited to personal financial gain or individual victimization. Nation-state actors and hacktivist groups have the power to disrupt critical infrastructure, causing widespread chaos and potentially endangering lives.

Imagine a scenario where an attack on a power grid plunges an entire city into darkness. Hospitals are unable to provide life-saving treatments, transportation systems grind to a halt, communication networks collapse, and essential services become inaccessible. This nightmare scenario is not far-fetched; it is a reality that we must be prepared for.

Critical infrastructure, including power grids, water supply systems, transportation networks, and communication systems, are all susceptible to cyber-attacks. The consequences of such attacks can have catastrophic effects on national security, public safety, and the economy.

Real-World Example: In 2015, Ukraine experienced one of the most significant cyber-attacks on its power grid. Hackers successfully infiltrated the control systems and cut off power to thousands of people. This attack served as a wake-up call for governments worldwide, highlighting the vulnerability of critical infrastructure to cyber-attacks.

Conclusion

The real-life consequences of cyber-attacks are no joke, and we can no longer afford to ignore the importance of cybersecurity. Financial losses, identity theft, reputation damage, and critical infrastructure disruption are just a few of the ways cyber-attacks can impact our lives. We must take proactive measures to protect our digital assets, educate ourselves and our communities about cybersecurity, and demand accountability from those responsible for our online safety.

Remember, it's not just about protecting your own shit; it's about safeguarding our collective digital future. So, get your cyber-defense game on, because in the Wild West of the digital realm, cybercriminals are always lurking, waiting for their next victim. Will it be you? Well, not if you give a shit about cybersecurity!

Why Gen-Z Needs to Give a Shit About Cybersecurity

Alright, listen up, you tech-savvy Gen-Z peeps. I know you're probably busy snapping selfies, swiping left and right on dating apps, and binge-watching the latest Netflix series, but I'm here to tell you why you need to give a serious shit about cybersecurity. Yeah, I said it. Cybersecurity affects every aspect of your life in the digital age, from your personal privacy to your online reputation, and even your financial security. So let's break it down and understand why this stuff matters to you.

First things first, let's talk about privacy. Now, I know you're no stranger to oversharing on social media. But here's the deal: your personal information is worth gold to cybercriminals and data collectors. Every time you post a selfie, comment on a friend's post, or fill out an online survey, you're leaving a digital footprint that can be used to track you, target you, or even steal your identity. And trust me, you don't want someone pretending to be you and wreaking havoc on your life.

But it's not just about your own privacy. By protecting your own digital shit, you're also protecting the privacy of others. Remember, we're all connected in this vast digital universe, and a chain is only as strong as its weakest link. So think twice before clicking on that shady link or sharing personal information with sketchy websites. You have the power to create a safer online space for everyone.

And what about your online reputation? Yeah, I know, you're too cool to care about what others think of you. But believe me, a tarnished online reputation can come back to bite you in the ass. We live in a world where future employers, college admissions officers, and even potential dates can easily Google your name and dig up all sorts of dirt on you. So be smart, my fellow Gen-Zers. Think before you post, tweet, or comment. That embarrassing drunk photo might seem funny now, but it could haunt you for years to come.

Now, let's talk money. I know that's something you all care about. Cybercriminals aren't just after your embarrassing selfies; they want your cold hard cash too. With the rise of online banking, mobile payments, and e-commerce, our financial lives have moved into the digital realm. But that also means that cybercriminals have more opportunities to steal your hard-earned money. From phishing scams to credit card skimmers, they're constantly coming up with new ways to trick you into handing over your cash. So, learn to spot the signs of a scam, protect your online banking credentials like your life depends on it, and check your financial statements regularly for any suspicious activity. Bank accounts should be sacred, not a free-for-all for hackers.

Alright, I've given you a good dose of reality. But here's the thing, cybersecurity isn't just about doom and gloom. It's also an exciting and ever-evolving field with plenty of career opportunities. As a Gen-Zer, you've grown up in a world where technology is an integral part of daily life. You understand the ins and outs of the digital landscape better than anyone else. So why not use that knowledge to your advantage? By diving into the world of cybersecurity, you can become a digital superhero. Imagine yourself as a hacker with a conscience, fighting against cybercriminals and protecting innocent people from falling victim to their schemes. Sounds pretty badass, right?

But you don't have to become a full-on hacker to make a difference. Cybersecurity professionals come in all shapes and sizes. Whether you're analyzing data breaches, investigating cybercrimes, or helping organizations beef up their security, there's a role out there that suits your skills and interests. Plus, with the increase in cyber threats, the job market for cybersecurity experts is booming. So, not only will you be doing something meaningful, but you'll also have a secure and well-paying job. That's a win-win situation if you ask me.

Alright, now that you're convinced that cybersecurity is worth giving a shit about, it's time to take action. Start by educating yourself on the basics of cybersecurity. Stay informed about the latest threats, learn how to spot phishing attempts, and understand the importance of creating strong, unique passwords.

Share your knowledge with your friends and family, because as I said earlier, the strength of our digital defense depends on all of us.

And don't forget that cybersecurity is an ongoing battle. It never stops evolving, and neither should your efforts to protect yourself and others. So, stay curious, keep learning, and always give a shit about cybersecurity. Because if you don't, the cyber criminals out there are ready and waiting to make your digital life a living hell. And trust me, you don't want that.

Resources: - "The Art of Invisibility: The World's Most Famous Hacker Teaches You How to Be Safe in the Age of Big Brother and Big Data" by Kevin Mitnick - "Click Here to Kill Everybody: Security and Survival in a Hyper-connected World" by Bruce Schneier - "Introduction to Computer Security" by Matt Bishop

Exercise: 1. Watch the documentary "The Great Hack" on Netflix and write a short reflection on how it changed your perspective on the importance of cybersecurity.

Remember, beloved Gen-Zers, the choices you make today will impact your digital future. So, embrace the world of cybersecurity, take control of your digital shit, and show the cybercriminals who's boss. Stay safe out there, and always give a shit about cybersecurity.

Debunking Common Misconceptions About Cybersecurity

Cybersecurity is a topic that is often misunderstood and shrouded in misconceptions. In this section, we will take a closer look at some of the most common misconceptions about cybersecurity and debunk them with clear explanations and examples. By debunking these misconceptions, we hope to provide you with a better understanding of the realities and importance of cybersecurity in the digital age.

Misconception #1: "I'm Just an Ordinary Person, Hackers Won't Target Me"

One of the biggest misconceptions about cybersecurity is that only high-profile individuals or large corporations are targeted by hackers. The truth is, anyone can be a target. Hackers cast a wide net and often exploit vulnerabilities in commonly used software or devices, without specifically targeting individuals. They use automated tools to scan the internet for vulnerable systems, and if they find one, they will exploit it.

For example, consider the case of a small business owner who believes that their business is too small to attract hackers' attention. They may not have robust cybersecurity measures in place, making them an easy target for cybercriminals. Once compromised, the hacker can steal sensitive customer information or use the business's resources for illegal activities.

Therefore, it is important to understand that cybersecurity threats do not discriminate based on individual status or organization size. Every individual and business must take steps to protect their digital assets.

Misconception #2: "I Only Need Antivirus Software to Stay Safe"

While antivirus software is an essential part of a cybersecurity defense strategy, it is not a silver bullet. Many people believe that having antivirus software installed on their devices means they are completely protected from all cyber threats. Unfortunately, this is not the case.

Antivirus software primarily focuses on detecting and removing known malware and viruses. It relies on signature-based detection methods to identify malware based on pre-existing patterns. However, cybercriminals are constantly evolving their attack techniques, creating new malware strains that can bypass traditional antivirus software.

Additionally, antivirus software cannot protect against other types of cyber threats, such as social engineering attacks or zero-day exploits. These types of attacks target human vulnerabilities or exploit unknown vulnerabilities in software, making traditional antivirus software ineffective.

To stay truly safe, individuals and organizations need to adopt a multi-layered approach to cybersecurity. This includes regularly updating software and operating systems, using strong and unique passwords, implementing two-factor authentication, and educating themselves about the latest cyber threats.

Misconception #3: "Using Public Wi-Fi is Safe as Long as I Don't Share Personal Information"

Many people believe that using public Wi-Fi networks is safe as long as they avoid sharing personal information such as passwords or credit card details. However, this is a common misconception that can expose users to significant cybersecurity risks.

Public Wi-Fi networks are often insecure and can be easily compromised by hackers. They can set up fake networks that mimic legitimate ones, known as "evil twin" attacks, to intercept users' data or spread malware. In such attacks, even if you don't share personal information, simply connecting to the network can expose your device to hacking attempts.

For instance, imagine you're sitting at a coffee shop and connecting to the free Wi-Fi. The network might appear to be legitimate, but it's actually set up by a hacker. They can eavesdrop on your online activities, capture your login credentials for various websites, or even inject malicious code into the web pages you visit.

To protect yourself when using public Wi-Fi, it's important to use a virtual private network (VPN) to encrypt your internet traffic. A VPN creates a secure connection between your device and the internet, making it difficult for hackers to intercept your data. Additionally, avoid accessing sensitive information or logging into important accounts when connected to public Wi-Fi networks.

Misconception #4: "Strong Passwords Are Enough to Protect My Accounts"

While it's true that using strong passwords is an important part of maintaining good cybersecurity hygiene, they are not a foolproof solution. Many people believe that by using complex passwords, they are immune to hacking attempts. However, cybercriminals have various methods at their disposal to crack passwords, such as brute-force attacks or using stolen password databases.

For example, let's say you have a strong password that is a long string of random characters. Despite its complexity, if a hacker gains access to the service you're using and finds that they have stored passwords in an insecure manner, they might be able to retrieve your password and use it to compromise your account on other platforms.

To enhance password security, it is important to follow best practices such as using unique passwords for each account, regularly changing passwords, and storing passwords in a reputable password manager. Implementing two-factor authentication adds an extra layer of security by requiring a second form of verification, such as a fingerprint scan or a one-time code.

By addressing these common misconceptions, we hope to bring awareness to the importance of cybersecurity and the need for proactive measures to protect ourselves in the digital wild west. Remember, cybersecurity is not a one-time fix, but an ongoing effort to stay vigilant and adapt to the evolving threat landscape. So, let's kick some cyber-ass and protect our digital shit!

Summary

In this section, we debunked several common misconceptions about cybersecurity. We highlighted the fact that individuals of all statuses can be targeted by hackers, emphasized the need for a multi-layered defense strategy beyond just antivirus software, explained the risks of using public Wi-Fi networks, and addressed the limitations of strong passwords.

It is essential to recognize that cybersecurity is a continuous process that requires constant vigilance and proactive measures. By debunking these misconceptions, we hope to empower readers with the knowledge and awareness necessary to protect their digital assets effectively.

Remember, in the digital wild west, everyone is a potential target, and it's up to us to defend our shit! Stay safe, stay vigilant, and stay informed.

The Role of Individuals in Protecting Their Digital Shit

In this digital age, where cyber threats lurk around every corner, it's crucial for individuals to take responsibility for protecting their digital shit. Yes, you heard it right, your shit! Your personal information, financial data, online accounts, and other digital assets are all at risk. But fear not, my Gen-Z friends, because I'm about to drop some knowledge bombs on how you can defend yourself in this wild cyber world.

First things first, let's understand why individuals should give a shit about cybersecurity. It's not just about protecting your own data (although that's important too), it's about preventing a domino effect. When one person's security is compromised, it can have a ripple effect, affecting others in their network. So, by protecting yourself, you're also protecting your friends, family, and even your favorite influencers.

Now, let's debunk some common misconceptions about cybersecurity. You might think, "I'm a small fish in this big cyber pond, who would bother hacking me?" Well, my friend, cybercriminals don't discriminate. They'll take down anyone who's an easy target. And guess what? You might actually be an easy target if you don't take precautions.

So, what role do you play in this cybersecurity game? It's time to step up and become the hero of your own digital fortress.

1. Stay updated on the latest threats: The digital landscape evolves at lightning speed. Stay informed about the latest cyber threats, scams, and hacking techniques. Follow trusted cybersecurity blogs, news outlets, and social media accounts. Knowledge is power, my friend.

2. Use strong and unique passwords: This might seem like a no-brainer, but you'd be surprised how many people still use "password123" as their go-to. Come on, you can do better than that! Create strong, unique, and hard-to-guess passwords

for all your online accounts. And no, using the same password for everything is not an option.

3. Enable two-factor authentication (2FA): Add an extra layer of security by enabling 2FA wherever possible. This could be a text message code, an email confirmation, or even a biometric scan. It might take a few extra seconds to log in, but trust me, it's worth it.

4. Be cautious of phishing attempts: Phishing is like the sneaky pickpocket of the cyber world. Cybercriminals will try to trick you into revealing your personal information through deceptive emails, websites, or messages. Be vigilant and verify the source before clicking on any links or sharing sensitive information.

5. Keep your software up to date: Those software update notifications might feel like a nuisance, but they're actually crucial for your security. Software updates often include patches and fixes that address vulnerabilities that cybercriminals can exploit. So, don't ignore those update reminders, my friend.

6. Think before you click: In the wild west of the digital world, not everything is as it seems. Think twice before clicking on suspicious links, downloading sketchy files, or opening random email attachments. It's better to be safe than sorry.

7. Educate yourself and others: Spread the knowledge, my friend. Educate yourself about cybersecurity best practices and share that knowledge with your friends, family, and even your teachers. The more people who give a shit about cybersecurity, the safer we'll all be.

Now, I know this might sound overwhelming, but hey, we're in this together. Remember, cybersecurity is a team effort. By taking simple steps to protect your digital shit, you're contributing to the larger goal of creating a safer online world for everyone.

So, my fellow Gen-Z warriors, let's gear up, lock down our digital fortresses, and kick some cyber-ass!

The Evolution of Cybercrime

From Sneaky Hackers to Cyber Gangsters

In the early days of cybersecurity, hackers were seen as sneaky individuals who used their skills to exploit vulnerabilities in computer systems. They were often motivated by curiosity or a desire to test the limits of technology. These hackers, or "white hats," focused on finding and fixing security flaws in order to protect systems from potential threats.

However, over time, the landscape of cybercrime has evolved dramatically. Today, we face a new breed of cyber gangsters who operate with malicious intent and are motivated by personal gain. These cybercriminals, or "black hats," have turned hacking into a lucrative underground business.

The Motives of Cyber Gangsters

Unlike their predecessors, these cyber gangsters are driven by financial gain. They exploit vulnerabilities in computer systems and networks to steal sensitive information, such as credit card numbers, personal identities, or intellectual property. They may then sell this information on the dark web, where it can be used for various illegal activities, including identity theft, fraud, or even espionage.

Some cyber gangsters operate in organized groups, known as cybercrime syndicates, which resemble modern-day digital mafia. These syndicates are well-coordinated and often have global reach, making it challenging for law enforcement to track them down.

The Tools and Techniques of Cyber Gangsters

Just as technology has advanced, so too have the tools and techniques employed by cyber gangsters. They use sophisticated hacking methods that exploit both technical vulnerabilities and human weaknesses. Some common techniques include:

- **Malware:** Cyber gangsters use malicious software, such as viruses, worms, and ransomware, to gain unauthorized access to computer systems. They may use phishing emails or infected websites to distribute malware, tricking unsuspecting users into opening the door to their digital fortress.

- **Botnets:** Cyber gangsters harness the power of botnets, which are networks of infected computers controlled remotely. These botnets can be used to launch large-scale attacks, such as distributed denial-of-service (DDoS) attacks, which overwhelm targeted systems with a flood of network traffic, causing them to become inaccessible.

- **Social engineering:** Cyber gangsters often rely on social engineering techniques to manipulate individuals into revealing sensitive information or performing actions that could compromise their security. This can involve impersonating trusted entities, such as banks or government agencies, through email or phone communication, in order to deceive victims.

The Economic Impact of Cyber Gangsters

The rise of cyber gangsters has had a significant economic impact on individuals, businesses, and even governments. The costs associated with cybercrime include financial losses from stolen funds, intellectual property theft, and the expenses incurred in responding to and recovering from cyber-attacks.

Furthermore, cyber-attacks can disrupt critical infrastructures, such as power grids or transportation systems, leading to significant financial and social consequences. The WannaCry ransomware attack in 2017, for example, affected thousands of organizations worldwide, including hospitals and government agencies, causing massive disruptions and financial losses.

Fighting Back Against Cyber Gangsters

Combating cyber gangsters requires a multi-faceted approach that involves both technical and legal measures. Here are some strategies to defend against their attacks:

- **Security Awareness:** Educating individuals and organizations about the risks and best practices in cybersecurity is crucial. By promoting a cybersecurity mindset and fostering a culture of responsible digital behavior, we can minimize the chances of falling victim to cyber gangsters' tactics.

- **Strong Security Measures:** Implementing robust security measures, such as regularly updating software, using strong and unique passwords, and enabling two-factor authentication, can thwart many hacking attempts.

- **Collaboration:** Sharing information about cyber threats and attacks among organizations and across borders is essential. By working together, we can stay one step ahead of cyber gangsters and better protect ourselves and our digital assets.

- **Legislation and Law Enforcement:** Governments play a critical role in combating cybercrime by enacting legislation that punishes cyber gangsters and strengthens victims' rights. Law enforcement agencies must also have the proper tools and resources to investigate and prosecute cybercriminals effectively.

It is important for individuals, organizations, and governments to work together in the fight against cyber gangsters. By staying informed, adopting strong security practices, and supporting initiatives that promote cybersecurity, we can collectively create a safer digital world.

Remember, in the Wild West of the internet, cyber gangsters may lurk in the shadows, but with knowledge and vigilance, we can keep our digital shit safe and secure.

The Rise of Nation-State Attacks

In the ever-evolving landscape of cyber threats, one of the most concerning developments is the rise of nation-state attacks. Traditionally, cybercrime has been associated with individual hackers or criminal organizations looking to make a quick buck. However, in recent years, state-sponsored cyberattacks have become increasingly common and pose a significant threat to individuals, businesses, and even national security.

The Motivation Behind Nation-State Attacks

Nation-state attacks, also known as cyber espionage or cyber warfare, are carried out by governments or state-affiliated entities with the aim of gathering intelligence, disrupting critical infrastructure, or engaging in covert activities. The motivations behind these attacks can be diverse and complex, including political, economic, military, and ideological objectives.

One of the primary motivations for nation-state attacks is the quest for strategic advantage. Governments engage in cyber espionage to gain insights into their adversaries' military capabilities, diplomatic strategies, and economic activities. By infiltrating foreign networks and stealing classified information, these states can gain a competitive edge and strengthen their position on the global stage.

Economic espionage is another significant driver of nation-state attacks. State-sponsored hackers target commercial enterprises to steal proprietary information, trade secrets, and intellectual property. This stolen data can be used to benefit domestic industries, create unfair advantages, or undermine foreign competitors. Examples of such attacks include the notorious hack on Sony Pictures Entertainment by North Korea in 2014 and the theft of intellectual property from US and European companies by Chinese state-sponsored hackers.

Some nation-states also use cyberattacks as a means of political coercion or sabotage. By targeting critical infrastructure, such as power grids, transportation systems, or financial networks, they can disrupt services and cause chaos, exerting pressure on their adversaries or advancing their own political agenda. For instance, the 2015 attack on Ukraine's power grid, attributed to Russian hackers, left parts of the country without electricity for several hours, sending a clear message of dominance and destabilization.

Methods and Techniques of Nation-State Attacks

Nation-state attacks are typically sophisticated and well-coordinated, employing advanced techniques and leveraging significant resources. These attackers often have access to cutting-edge tools, zero-day vulnerabilities, and extensive intelligence resources, making them formidable adversaries.

One common method used in nation-state attacks is advanced persistent threats (APTs). APTs involve a prolonged and stealthy compromise of a target network, with the goal of remaining undetected for an extended period. Attackers gain a foothold by exploiting vulnerabilities, using spear-phishing techniques, or deploying malware that evades traditional security measures. Once inside the network, they conduct reconnaissance, progressively escalating their privileges, and exfiltrating sensitive information.

Another technique employed by nation-state attackers is "watering hole" attacks. In this approach, hackers compromise websites that are likely to be visited by their intended targets. By injecting malicious code into these legitimate websites, attackers can silently infect the devices of their victims, gaining unauthorized access to their systems and data.

Zero-day exploits, which are undisclosed vulnerabilities in software or hardware, are highly valuable assets for nation-state attackers. These vulnerabilities, when discovered and exploited, give the attackers a significant advantage since there are no patches or defenses available. Nation-states often keep these vulnerabilities secret and use them strategically to breach targeted systems or gain unauthorized access to sensitive information.

State-sponsored attacks also frequently involve the use of malware specifically designed for espionage or sabotage. These include keyloggers, remote access trojans (RATs), and rootkits that allow attackers to monitor and control compromised systems, steal data, or launch further attacks. Such malware is meticulously crafted to evade detection and maintain persistence within the target environment.

Attribution Challenges and Geopolitical Implications

One of the significant challenges in dealing with nation-state attacks is the issue of attribution. Unlike individual hackers or criminal organizations, nation-states have the resources and capabilities to conceal their identities and launch attacks through proxy servers, compromised infrastructure, or other obfuscation techniques. This makes it difficult to definitively attribute an attack to a specific nation-state, leading to speculation and diplomatic tensions.

The geopolitical implications of nation-state attacks are far-reaching. They can strain international relationships, raise concerns about sovereignty and security, and even spark conflicts. In recent years, several high-profile incidents have strained diplomatic relations between countries and escalated tensions. For example, the cyberattacks on the Democratic National Committee during the 2016 US presidential election, attributed to Russian hackers, fueled allegations of interference and prompted retaliatory measures.

Moreover, the proliferation of nation-state attacks poses a challenge to the norms and principles that govern cyberspace. There is an ongoing debate about the rules of engagement in cyberspace and the applicability of existing international laws and treaties to cyber warfare. The lack of consensus on these issues complicates efforts to establish norms of responsible behavior among nation-states and mitigate the risks of escalating cyber conflicts.

Countering Nation-State Attacks

Addressing the threat of nation-state attacks requires a multi-faceted approach that encompasses technical, legal, and diplomatic measures. Some of the key strategies for countering these attacks include:

1. Strengthening Defenses: Organizations and individuals must implement robust cybersecurity measures, including network segmentation, endpoint protection, and intrusion detection systems. Regular patching, security awareness training, and incident response planning are crucial in mitigating the risk of nation-state attacks.

2. Information Sharing and Collaboration: Close collaboration between private sector organizations, government agencies, and international partners is essential in defending against nation-state attacks. Sharing threat intelligence, best practices, and incident response strategies can enhance collective resilience.

3. Diplomacy and International Cooperation: Formulating and promoting international norms, treaties, and agreements pertaining to cybersecurity is crucial for establishing boundaries and deterring malicious behavior by nation-states. Engaging in diplomatic dialogue and fostering cooperation can contribute to building trust and reducing the likelihood of cyber conflicts.

4. Investing in Research and Development: It is essential to allocate resources to research and development efforts aimed at enhancing cybersecurity capabilities and strengthening defenses against evolving nation-state attack techniques. Encouraging

innovation and supporting cybersecurity education and training programs can foster a skilled workforce capable of combating these threats.

While countering nation-state attacks is a challenging task, it is vital for the security and stability of cyberspace. By understanding the motivations, techniques, and implications of these attacks, individuals and organizations can take proactive steps to protect their digital assets and stay one step ahead of state-sponsored hackers.

Summary

In summary, nation-state attacks are a significant and evolving threat in the realm of cybersecurity. Motivated by strategic, economic, and political objectives, these attacks can have severe repercussions on both individuals and nations. Nation-state attackers employ sophisticated techniques, exploit vulnerabilities, and use advanced malware to compromise target systems. The challenge of attribution and the geopolitical implications associated with these attacks further complicate efforts to combat them effectively. Countering nation-state attacks requires strong defenses, collaboration, international cooperation, and investments in research and development. By taking proactive measures and understanding the nature of this threat, individuals and organizations can better protect themselves in the digital wild west of cyberspace.

The Dark Web: Where Illegal Sh*t Goes Down

Alright, buckle up, boys and girls. We're about to take a deep dive into the seedy underbelly of the internet - the Dark Web. It's the virtual equivalent of your favorite crime-infested neighborhood, the place where all the shady characters go to do their dirty business. In this section, we'll explore the less savory side of the cyber world and uncover what goes on when the lights go out.

Unmasking the Dark Web

Before we dive headfirst into this digital abyss, let's get one thing straight: the Dark Web is not the same as the surface web we all know and love. It's like comparing a cute little kitten to a ferocious lion. You see, the surface web is what you access every day when you search for cat videos or fill up your shopping cart on Amazon. It's all the websites that search engines like Google can find and index.

But the Dark Web? Oh boy, it's a whole different beast. It's a hidden part of the internet, accessible only through special software that allows users to remain anonymous and untraceable. Think of it as a secret club for cyber criminals, where they can buy and sell illegal goods, exchange sensitive information, and plan nefarious activities. To connect to the Dark Web, you need to use Tor (short for The Onion Router), which bounces your internet connection through a series of random computers around the world, making it nearly impossible to track.

Now, let's put our detective hats on and explore some of the shady places you might stumble upon while wandering through the Dark Web.

Black Markets and the Sale of Contraband

If you thought your local drug dealer was dodgy, wait till you see what's happening on the Dark Web. This digital underground is bustling with black markets where everything from drugs and counterfeit money to stolen credit card information and firearms are up for sale. It's like eBay for criminals, a one-stop shop for all your illegal needs.

One infamous example of a Dark Web marketplace is the now-defunct Silk Road. Created by the enigmatic Ross Ulbricht, a.k.a. Dread Pirate Roberts, Silk Road became a digital haven for drug dealers worldwide. It operated similar to any e-commerce site, complete with user ratings and reviews, but instead of buying a new pair of sneakers, users could score a bag of cocaine or even hire an assassin (yes, seriously).

Although Silk Road was eventually shut down by the FBI, countless other black markets have taken its place. The Dark Web continues to serve as a thriving hub for the illicit trade, making it a constant headache for law enforcement agencies trying to keep up.

Hacking Tools and Services

The Dark Web isn't just a marketplace for physical goods. It's also a treasure trove for cybercriminals looking for tools of the trade. Need a powerful hacking tool to infiltrate a secure network? No problem, just head to the Dark Web and take your pick.

You'll find an array of hacking tools, software exploits, and even tutorials on how to carry out a successful cyber attack. It's like a hacker's paradise, with an entire ecosystem dedicated to helping them wreak havoc on the digital landscape.

But not all Dark Web users are malicious hackers. Some are cybersecurity professionals who want to stay one step ahead of the bad guys. They visit the Dark Web to gather intelligence, learn about new vulnerabilities, and understand emerging cyber threats. It's an unconventional strategy, but in this never-ending arms race between hackers and cybersecurity professionals, sometimes you have to fight fire with fire.

Whistleblowing and Freedom of Speech

Amidst all the crime and chaos, there is a glimmer of hope on the Dark Web. It provides a platform for whistleblowers and activists to share sensitive information without fear of reprisal.

Take, for example, WikiLeaks. Love it or hate it, WikiLeaks has used the Dark Web to release classified documents and expose government secrets. By maintaining anonymity and avoiding censorship, whistleblowers can shine a light on corruption, sparking debates and holding the powerful accountable.

The Dark Web also plays a crucial role in countries where freedom of speech is severely restricted. Journalists, activists, and everyday people who dare to challenge oppressive regimes can use this hidden corner of the internet to voice their opinions and share information that would otherwise be censored or punished.

The Dark Side: Online Extremism and Illegal Activities

Unfortunately, not all Dark Web activities are so noble. The anonymity provided by the Dark Web has allowed extremist groups to thrive online, spreading hate speech, radicalizing vulnerable individuals, and plotting acts of violence. It's a digital breeding ground for terrorists and extremists, making it a virtual battleground for law enforcement agencies across the globe.

Furthermore, the Dark Web is fertile ground for illegal pornography, human trafficking, and other heinous crimes. These despicable activities thrive in the shadows, offering anonymity for those who engage in such repugnant behavior.

Staying Out of the Abyss

Now that you have a glimpse into the dark and murky world of the Dark Web, it's crucial to know how to protect yourself from its dangers. Here are a few key takeaways to ensure you don't get sucked into the abyss:

- Stay the hell away: There's really no need to delve into the Dark Web unless you have a legitimate reason (and the necessary skills) to do so. Curiosity killed the cat, my friend.

- Strengthen your defenses: Make sure your devices are protected with up-to-date antivirus software and firewalls. Enable automatic updates and practice good cybersecurity hygiene.

- Use unique passwords: Don't use the same damn password for every online account. Come up with strong and unique passwords for each site, and consider using a password manager to keep track of them all.
- Be a smart surfer: Avoid shady websites like you avoid your creepy neighbor. Stick to reputable sites, and don't click on suspicious links or download unknown files.
- Never share too much: Be cautious about what personal information you share online, especially on social media. Keep your digital footprint small and your privacy intact.

Remember, the Dark Web may be fascinating from afar, but it's a dangerous place where illegal sh*t goes down. So, stay safe, be smart, and keep your digital fortress impenetrable.

And with that, our glimpse into the forbidden realm of the Dark Web comes to an end. But fear not, there's still plenty more to learn about cybersecurity. So, buckle up, my friends, because we're just getting started.

Cybersecurity Challenges in the Digital Wild West

Welcome to the tumultuous world of cybersecurity, where we ride through the digital wild west, facing an ever-growing horde of cyber threats. In this section, we will explore the unique challenges that this digital frontier presents and equip you with the knowledge and tools needed to navigate this treacherous landscape.

The Changing Face of Cybercrime

As technology evolves, so does the nature of cybercrime. Gone are the days when hackers hid in the shadows, operating in isolation. Today, cybercriminals have adopted a more sinister approach, collaborating in hacking communities and sharing tools and tactics on the dark web.

The digital wild west is no longer just a place for sneaky hackers—now it's infested with cyber gangsters. These organized crime groups utilize sophisticated techniques and exploit vulnerabilities in our increasingly interconnected world. They weaponize technology to launch large-scale attacks that can disrupt critical infrastructure, compromise sensitive data, and cause substantial financial losses.

Furthermore, the rise of nation-state attacks adds another layer of complexity to the cyber landscape. Governments and intelligence agencies utilize advanced cyber espionage techniques to gather intelligence, disrupt enemy operations, and wage cyber warfare.

Navigating the Dark Web

One of the most dangerous and lawless frontiers in the digital wild west is the dark web. Operating on encrypted networks like Tor, the dark web provides an anonymous haven for illegal activities. It hosts marketplaces where cybercriminals buy and sell stolen data, malware, and hacking tools.

Law enforcement agencies face significant challenges in tackling cybercrime on the dark web. The decentralized nature of these networks, combined with strong encryption, makes it difficult to trace and apprehend cybercriminals. As a result, the digital wild west has become a breeding ground for cybercrime, with criminals operating with near-impunity.

The Cat and Mouse Game

In the digital wild west, cybersecurity professionals constantly find themselves engaged in an intense arms race with hackers. As organizations fortify their defenses, cybercriminals evolve their tactics to breach these barriers. It's a never-ending cat and mouse game, with both sides implementing new techniques and strategies to outsmart each other.

For instance, hackers employ advanced techniques like social engineering to manipulate unsuspecting individuals and gain unauthorized access to systems. They exploit human vulnerabilities, such as trust and curiosity, to deceive individuals into divulging sensitive information or clicking on malicious links.

In response, cybersecurity professionals must continually stay up-to-date with the latest attack vectors and develop countermeasures to protect against them. This includes implementing robust security measures, conducting regular vulnerability assessments, and educating individuals about potential threats and best practices.

The Human Element: A Weak Link

Despite technological advancements, humans remain the weakest link in the cybersecurity chain. Cybercriminals understand this and exploit the human element through various tactics, like phishing attacks and social engineering.

Phishing attacks involve sending fraudulent emails that appear to come from trustworthy sources, enticing individuals to reveal sensitive information or download malicious files. Social engineering tactics prey on human psychology, manipulating individuals into divulging confidential information or granting unauthorized access.

To defend against such attacks, individuals need to be vigilant and develop a healthy skepticism towards unsolicited emails, suspicious links, and unfamiliar requests for personal information. Organizations also play a crucial role in building a strong security culture by providing cybersecurity awareness training and implementing robust policies and procedures.

The Regulatory Maze

In the digital wild west, navigating the legal and regulatory landscape can be as challenging as defending against cyber threats. Governments around the world have recognized the need for cybersecurity regulations to protect individuals and organizations from cyber attacks.

However, the ever-changing nature of technology and the global reach of cybercrime create unique challenges in creating effective regulations. Balancing the need for security with individual privacy rights, while also accounting for the rapid pace of technological advancements, is no easy feat.

As a result, cybersecurity professionals must stay informed about relevant laws and regulations in their operating jurisdictions. Compliance with these regulations is not only ethically and legally necessary but also a vital component of an organization's cybersecurity strategy.

The Call to Action

The digital wild west presents a host of challenges that demand our attention and action. Cybersecurity is not just a concern for governments and organizations; as individuals living in the digital age, we must also take responsibility for protecting our digital shit.

In the following sections, we will delve into the practical aspects of cybersecurity, equipping you with the knowledge and tools to secure your digital fortress. By taking proactive steps to protect your digital assets, you can minimize the risk of falling victim to cybercrime and contribute to the collective effort of taming the digital wild west.

But first, let's bust some myths and misconceptions about cybersecurity in the next section—because without dispelling the bullshit, you can't build a solid foundation of knowledge. So saddle up, partner, and let's ride into the world of cybersecurity debunkery!

The Arms Race: Hackers vs. Cybersecurity Professionals

In the vast and lawless landscape of the cyber world, a never-ending arms race is being waged between hackers and cybersecurity professionals. This battle between those who seek to exploit vulnerabilities and those who strive to protect our digital shit is constantly evolving, with each side racing to outsmart the other. In this section, we will explore the dynamics of this arms race, the tactics employed by both hackers and cybersecurity professionals, and the challenges they face.

Understanding the Hacker Mindset

To understand the arms race, we must first delve into the hacker mindset. Hackers are individuals who possess a deep understanding of computer systems and exploit vulnerabilities to gain unauthorized access or cause damage. They are driven by various motivations, including financial gain, ideology, curiosity, or the sheer thrill of the challenge.

Hackers employ a wide range of techniques to compromise systems and exploit weaknesses. They often use social engineering tactics to deceive individuals or gain their trust, or they can exploit software vulnerabilities to gain unauthorized access. Some hackers specialize in specific areas, such as network hacking, web application hacking, or malware development.

The Role of Cybersecurity Professionals

On the other side of the battlefield are the cybersecurity professionals. These individuals are dedicated to defending digital systems and protecting sensitive data from malicious attacks. They employ various strategies, tools, and technologies to safeguard against hackers and minimize potential risks.

Cybersecurity professionals work tirelessly to stay one step ahead of hackers. They analyze the tactics and techniques used by hackers, identify vulnerabilities, and develop countermeasures to protect against them. This involves constantly monitoring and updating systems, implementing strong security protocols, and educating users on best practices.

The Cat-and-Mouse Game

The arms race between hackers and cybersecurity professionals resembles a cat-and-mouse game, with each side continuously adapting to the other's tactics. Hackers discover new vulnerabilities or develop more sophisticated attack techniques, while cybersecurity professionals devise defensive measures to patch vulnerabilities and mitigate threats.

One common tactic employed by hackers is the use of zero-day exploits. Zero-day exploits are vulnerabilities that are previously unknown to software vendors, giving hackers an advantage. As soon as these vulnerabilities are discovered, cybersecurity professionals race against the clock to develop patches and prevent potential attacks.

Emerging Technologies and the Arms Race

The arms race is further fueled by emerging technologies that pose new challenges for both hackers and cybersecurity professionals. For example, the increasing adoption of Internet of Things (IoT) devices introduces a vast array of potential vulnerabilities. Hackers can target these devices to gain entry into networks or even launch large-scale attacks.

Another area of concern is the growing sophistication of artificial intelligence (AI) and machine learning (ML) algorithms. While these technologies can be used to enhance cybersecurity defenses, they can also be employed by hackers to automate attacks and evade detection. Cybersecurity professionals must adapt their strategies and tools to keep pace with these advancements.

Collaboration and Information Sharing

In this high-stakes arms race, collaboration and information sharing play a crucial role. Cybersecurity professionals collaborate with one another, sharing information about new threats, attack techniques, and defense strategies. Sharing this knowledge helps the community stay informed and respond more effectively to emerging threats.

Bug bounties are another form of collaboration in the cybersecurity field. Organizations offer rewards to individuals who identify and report vulnerabilities in their systems. This incentivizes ethical hackers to contribute their expertise and helps organizations proactively identify and address vulnerabilities before malicious actors exploit them.

The Future of the Arms Race

Looking ahead, the arms race between hackers and cybersecurity professionals shows no signs of slowing down. As technology continues to advance, hackers will discover new ways to exploit vulnerabilities, and cybersecurity professionals will develop innovative strategies to defend against them.

Quantum computing is an area that holds both promise and concern. While quantum computing has the potential to revolutionize many fields, including cryptography, it also poses a threat to existing encryption systems. Cybersecurity professionals must stay ahead of the curve, researching and developing quantum-resistant encryption algorithms to ensure the security of sensitive data.

The arms race is a never-ending battle, but one that must be fought to protect our digital shit. As individuals, it is essential to maintain a vigilant mindset and adopt proactive measures to safeguard our personal information. By understanding the dynamics of the arms race and staying informed about emerging threats, we can all play a part in defending ourselves and contributing to the ever-evolving field of cybersecurity.

Exercise: Analyzing Real-World Hacking Attacks

1. Research and analyze a recent high-profile hacking attack. Identify the vulnerabilities that were exploited and the impact it had on the affected organization or individuals. Discuss the measures that could have been taken to prevent or mitigate the attack.

2. Imagine you are a cybersecurity professional tasked with securing a network against potential attacks. Identify the key areas of vulnerability and develop a comprehensive strategy to protect the network. Consider both technical measures (such as firewalls and encryption) and user education and awareness programs.

3. Conduct research on bug bounty programs offered by various organizations. Select one program and analyze its effectiveness in identifying vulnerabilities. Discuss the benefits and challenges of bug bounty programs in the context of the arms race between hackers and cybersecurity professionals.

4. Investigate the potential ethical dilemmas faced by cybersecurity professionals in their efforts to defend against attacks. Discuss situations in which the line between "white hat" and "black hat" activities becomes blurred. What factors should cybersecurity professionals consider when making ethical decisions?

Remember, in this digital wild west, the hackers are constantly evolving their tactics, and cybersecurity professionals must rise to the challenge. Stay informed, be vigilant, and be ready to defend your shit against those who seek to exploit it. Now, saddle up and let's ride into the next chapter of cybersecurity.

Ethical and Legal Considerations in Cybersecurity

The Fine Line Between White Hats and Black Hats

In the vast world of cybersecurity, there are two distinct groups of individuals who are constantly at odds with each other: the white hats and the black hats. These terms may sound like a bizarre fashion statement, but they actually refer to the ethical (or sometimes not-so-ethical) hackers who wield their skills and knowledge to either protect or exploit digital systems.

Defining White Hats and Black Hats

White hats, also known as ethical hackers or security researchers, are the good guys of the cyber world. They use their expertise to identify vulnerabilities in computer systems, networks, and software applications. Their ultimate goal is to help organizations and individuals protect themselves from cyber-attacks. Think of them as the digital superheroes who work tirelessly to safeguard our online lives.

On the other hand, black hats, also known as malicious hackers or cybercriminals, are the villains in this story. They exploit vulnerabilities in computer systems for personal gain, causing harm to individuals, organizations, or even entire nations. Their motivations can range from financial gain to political activism, but regardless of their reasons, their actions are considered illegal and unethical.

The Gray Area: Gray Hats

Now, let's throw in a little shade to make things more interesting. There is a gray area in the cybersecurity realm, known as gray hats. These individuals may not fit neatly into either the white hat or black hat category. They possess hacking skills and knowledge, but their motivations and actions can be ambiguous.

Gray hats may sometimes perform unauthorized actions to expose vulnerabilities in a system, with the intent of raising awareness and prompting the system owner to fix those vulnerabilities. While they may have good intentions, their methods still walk a fine line between ethical and illegal behavior. Some gray hats may eventually transition to becoming white hats, realizing the importance of responsible and legal hacking.

Ethics in Hacking

The key difference between white hats and black hats lies in their ethical considerations and the actions they take. White hats operate within legal boundaries and follow a strict code of ethics. They are driven by the desire to make the digital world a safer place and adhere to principles such as:

- Obtaining proper authorization before conducting any security assessment.

- Maintaining the confidentiality of any sensitive information discovered during their work.

- Sharing vulnerabilities and findings responsibly with the affected parties.

- Focusing on improving and protecting cybersecurity without causing harm or disruptions.

Black hats, on the other hand, throw these ethical principles out the window. They engage in illegal activities, such as unauthorized access, data theft, or denial-of-service attacks, all for personal gain or malicious intent.

Navigating the Fine Line

For those interested in a career in cybersecurity, it is essential to understand the boundaries between white and black hat activities. It's important to make ethical choices and stay on the right side of the law. Here are some guidelines to help you navigate this fine line:

- Obtain the necessary education and certifications to become a legitimate professional in the field.

- Familiarize yourself with laws and regulations regarding hacking and cybersecurity in your jurisdiction.

- Seek legal and ethical hacking opportunities, such as participating in bug bounty programs or joining security organizations that promote responsible hacking.

- Always obtain proper authorization before conducting any security assessment.

- Avoid using or creating hacking tools or techniques that can be used for illegal activities.

- Never engage in any activities that cause harm, disrupt systems, or violate the privacy of individuals without their consent.

- Report any vulnerabilities or findings to the respective organizations, following responsible disclosure practices.

While hacking can be an adrenaline-inducing and intellectually stimulating field, it is crucial to remember that the actions you take can have far-reaching consequences. By staying on the white hat side of the spectrum, you can make a positive impact and help create a safer digital world.

Case Study: The Gray Hat Hacker

Let's delve into a real-world example that highlights the complexity of the white hat vs. black hat debate.

In 2014, a talented hacker named Marcus Hutchins, also known as MalwareTech, inadvertently became a hero by stopping the spread of the WannaCry ransomware attack, which had already infected hundreds of thousands of computers worldwide. Marcus discovered a "kill switch" that disabled the ransomware, effectively halting its destructive path.

However, Marcus had a darker side to his hacking past. Before turning to white hat activities, he had involvement with the creation and dissemination of malware. This revelation raised questions about the fine line between white and black hat activities and whether someone with such a background could be trusted. Marcus's case illustrates the complexity of the hacker's journey and the ongoing debate surrounding redemption and forgiveness in the cybersecurity community.

Conclusion

In the ever-evolving landscape of cybersecurity, the distinction between white hats and black hats is crucial. White hats play a vital role in securing our digital world, while black hats pose a constant threat to individuals and organizations. Aspiring cybersecurity professionals must understand the ethical considerations and responsibilities that come with their chosen path. By embracing the white hat mindset, they can contribute to a safer digital future while staying on the right side of the law. So, choose your hat wisely and get ready to protect and defend in the digital wild west.

Ethics in Hacking: When to Cross the Line and When to Back the F*ck Off

In the realm of cybersecurity, hacking is often seen as a necessary tool in the fight against cybercrime. But where do we draw the line between ethical hacking and malicious attacks? In this section, we will explore the ethical considerations that hackers face and discuss when it is appropriate to cross the line and when it is essential to back the f*ck off.

Understanding the Hacker's Code

To navigate the complex world of hacking ethics, it is essential to understand the principles that guide many hackers. One fundamental code is the belief in the power of knowledge and the freedom to explore and experiment. Hackers value their ability to understand and uncover vulnerabilities, viewing it as a means to improve security rather than exploit it.

Another principle is the commitment to responsible disclosure. Ethical hackers follow a set of protocols when they discover vulnerabilities, allowing them to responsibly report those weaknesses to the appropriate parties. This ensures that the vulnerabilities are patched before they can be exploited by malicious actors.

Ethical Hacking vs. Malicious Attacks

Ethical hacking, also known as white hat hacking, refers to hacking activities conducted with the explicit permission of the system owner for the purpose of improving security. These hackers work within legal boundaries, often as part of a security team, to identify and fix vulnerabilities.

In contrast, malicious attacks, also known as black hat hacking, involve hacking without permission and with the intention to cause harm, steal information, or disrupt systems. These activities are illegal and punishable by law.

It is vital to differentiate between the two and understand the significant impact of hacking with good intentions versus hacking with malicious intent. Ethical hackers contribute to a safer digital world, while malicious hackers cause chaos and harm.

When to Cross the Line

While ethical hackers operate within legal boundaries, there are instances where they may need to push those boundaries to achieve their goals. Here are a few scenarios where crossing the line may be ethically justified:

- **Informed Consent:** If a system owner explicitly grants permission for security testing or penetration testing, ethical hackers can go beyond the usual boundaries to uncover vulnerabilities. However, it is essential to obtain written consent to avoid legal complications.

- **Emergency Situations:** Sometimes, in critical situations where lives or public safety are at risk, ethical hackers may need to cross legal boundaries temporarily to prevent or mitigate a cyber threat. However, extreme caution must be exercised to ensure actions are proportional and minimize potential harm.

- **Civil Disobedience:** In certain cases where malicious actors evade legal consequences due to legal loopholes or corruption, ethical hackers may engage in civil disobedience to expose these vulnerabilities and promote accountability. However, such actions should be the last resort and carried out responsibly without causing collateral damage.

It is crucial to note that even in cases where crossing the line may be ethically justified, hackers must be aware of the potential legal consequences. Consultation with legal experts is highly recommended to navigate these complex situations.

When to Back the F*ck Off

While ethical hacking allows for pushing boundaries, there are clear instances where it is essential to back the f*ck off. These situations include:

- **Unauthorized Access:** Without explicit permission, hacking into a system or network is illegal and unethical. Respecting the privacy and property rights of individuals and organizations is crucial.

- **Non-Consensual Monitoring:** Monitoring or intercepting someone's private communications without their consent is a severe violation of privacy and is both illegal and unethical. It is important to respect boundaries and obtain proper consent when accessing or monitoring data.

- **Harmful Exploitation:** Exploiting vulnerabilities to cause harm, steal sensitive data, or disrupt systems is strictly unethical. Ethical hackers work towards improving security, not exploiting it for personal gain or malicious intent.

It is essential to remember that hacking should always be approached with a sense of responsibility and a clear understanding of the ethical implications involved.

Exercises

Exercise 1

Consider the scenario where an ethical hacker discovers a critical vulnerability in a widely used software application. The software company has a reputation for being slow in addressing security issues. As an ethical hacker, what could you do to responsibly disclose the vulnerability and ensure it is addressed promptly? Discuss the steps you would take and the potential challenges you might face.

Exercise 2

Research and investigate a recent case where an individual engaged in hacking activities with malicious intent, causing significant harm to individuals or organizations. Analyze the motivations and consequences of their actions. Discuss what ethical hacking practices could have potentially prevented or mitigated the impact of these attacks.

Additional Resources

1. **Book:** "The Web Application Hacker's Handbook" by Dafydd Stuttard and Marcus Pinto. This comprehensive guide provides insights into ethical hacking techniques and methodologies, helping readers develop a deep understanding of web application vulnerabilities and secure coding practices.

2. **Website:** "Open Web Application Security Project (OWASP)" provides resources, tools, and guidelines for secure web application development. It also offers materials on ethical hacking and responsible disclosure practices.

3. **Online Course:** "Introduction to Ethical Hacking" on platforms like Coursera or Udemy. This course provides a structured introduction to ethical hacking principles, methodologies, and best practices, helping beginners gain essential knowledge and skills in a hands-on learning environment.

Remember, ethical hacking is a powerful tool that can make a positive impact on cybersecurity. By understanding the ethical considerations and choosing the right path, hackers can become defenders of the digital world, protecting our shit in the ever-expanding digital Wild West. So, choose wisely and always remember, hacking is a responsibility, not an excuse to be a f*cking asshat.

Cybersecurity Laws and Regulations: Navigating the Legal Maze

In the digital world, where cyber threats are lurking around every corner, it is essential to have a solid understanding of cybersecurity laws and regulations. Navigating the legal maze can be a daunting task, but it is crucial to protect yourself, your data, and your digital assets.

The Need for Cybersecurity Laws

With the increasing sophistication and frequency of cyber attacks, governments around the world have recognized the need for robust cybersecurity laws and regulations. These laws aim to establish a legal framework to protect individuals, businesses, and critical infrastructure from cyber threats.

The primary objectives of cybersecurity laws are:

- **Prevention:** Cybersecurity laws outline preventive measures that individuals and organizations should take to secure their digital systems and data.

- **Detection and Response:** Laws also address the mechanisms for detecting and responding to cyber threats, including incident reporting and coordination between various stakeholders.

- **Accountability and Liability:** Laws define the responsibilities and liabilities of individuals, organizations, and service providers in the event of a cyber incident or data breach.

- **Privacy Protection:** Cybersecurity laws also address the protection of individuals' privacy rights and regulate the collection, storage, and use of personal data.

Overview of Cybersecurity Laws and Regulations

Cybersecurity laws and regulations vary from country to country, but there are common principles and best practices that many jurisdictions follow. Here are some key areas covered by cybersecurity laws:

1. **Data Protection Laws:** These laws govern the collection, storage, and use of personal data by organizations. They often require obtaining consent from individuals, implementing security measures to protect data, and notifying individuals in case of a data breach.

2. **Computer Crime Laws:** Computer crime laws make certain activities illegal, such as unauthorized access to computer systems, hacking, and distributing malware. They also define the penalties for these offenses.

3. **Data Breach Notification Laws:** These laws require organizations to inform individuals, regulators, and other stakeholders about data breaches that may compromise their personal information. They typically outline the time frames and procedures for reporting such incidents.

4. **Industry-Specific Regulations:** Some sectors, such as healthcare and finance, have specific regulations that require additional cybersecurity measures due to the sensitivity of the data they handle. For example, the Health Insurance Portability and Accountability Act (HIPAA) in the United States sets standards for protecting medical information.

5. **International Cybersecurity Agreements:** Governments often collaborate on cybersecurity issues through international agreements. These agreements promote information sharing, cooperation in addressing cyber threats, and the development of common cybersecurity standards.

Examples of Cybersecurity Laws and Regulations

To better understand the practical application of cybersecurity laws, let's take a look at a few examples from different jurisdictions:

- **General Data Protection Regulation (GDPR) - European Union:** The GDPR is one of the most comprehensive data protection regulations globally. It applies to all organizations that handle the personal data of EU residents, regardless of the organization's location. The GDPR grants individuals greater control over their personal data, requires organizations to implement strict security measures, and imposes significant penalties for non-compliance.

- **California Consumer Privacy Act (CCPA) - United States:** The CCPA is a state-level data protection law that gives California residents more control over their personal information. It requires businesses to disclose their data collection and sharing practices, allows individuals to opt out of the sale of their data, and gives them the right to request the deletion of their personal data.

- **The Notifiable Data Breaches (NDB) Scheme - Australia:** The NDB scheme requires organizations covered by the Privacy Act 1988 to notify individuals and the Office of the Australian Information Commissioner (OAIC) when a data breach is likely to result in serious harm to individuals whose personal information is involved. This scheme aims to enhance transparency and encourage organizations to improve their data protection practices.

The Challenges of Cybersecurity Laws and Regulations

While cybersecurity laws and regulations play a vital role in mitigating cyber risks, they also face several challenges:

- **Rapid Technological Advancements:** Cybersecurity laws must keep pace with rapidly evolving technologies and emerging threats. It is challenging for legislators to draft laws that are both future-proof and flexible enough to adapt to changing circumstances.

- **Jurisdictional Issues:** The global nature of the internet poses challenges for jurisdictional enforcement. Cybercriminals can operate from one country while targeting victims in another. Cooperation among governments and international organizations is crucial to address these challenges.

- **Compliance and Enforcement:** Organizations often struggle with compliance due to the complexity and ever-changing nature of cybersecurity laws. Additionally, enforcing cybersecurity laws can be challenging, especially when dealing with cybercriminals operating from jurisdictions with lax cybersecurity regulations.

Staying Compliant with Cybersecurity Laws

To navigate the legal maze of cybersecurity laws and regulations effectively, here are some best practices:

- **Stay Informed:** Stay abreast of cybersecurity laws applicable to your jurisdiction and industry. Regularly consult reputable sources, such as government websites or legal experts, to ensure you are up to date with the latest regulations.

- **Implement Security Measures:** Take proactive steps to secure your digital systems and data. Implement strong access controls, encryption, and regular security assessments to mitigate the risk of cyber incidents.

- **Develop Incident Response Plans:** Prepare for potential cyber incidents by developing an incident response plan. This plan should outline the steps to be taken in the event of a breach, including notifying individuals and regulators as required by law.

- **Seek Legal Advice:** Consult legal professionals who specialize in cybersecurity to ensure compliance with relevant laws. They can provide valuable guidance on implementing security measures, drafting policies, and responding to incidents.

Conclusion

Cybersecurity laws and regulations are crucial for protecting individuals, organizations, and critical infrastructure from cyber threats. Navigating the legal maze can be complex, but understanding and complying with cybersecurity laws is essential in the digital age.

By staying informed, implementing security measures, developing incident response plans, and seeking legal advice when needed, you can navigate the legal landscape with confidence. Remember, cybersecurity is a shared responsibility, and adherence to laws and regulations is paramount in keeping our digital ecosystem safe and secure.

Privacy Rights in the Digital Age: How to Not Get F*cked Over

In today's digital world, privacy rights are more important than ever. With the constant advancement of technology, our personal data is more vulnerable to being exploited and our digital privacy is at risk. In this section, we will explore the challenges we face in maintaining our privacy in the digital age and provide strategies to protect ourselves from getting f*cked over.

Understanding Data Privacy

Data privacy refers to the protection of personal information that individuals share online. Your data, such as your name, address, social media activities, and browsing history, is valuable and should be treated as such. Unfortunately, many companies and organizations exploit our data to make a profit or gain an advantage. One example of this is targeted advertising, where companies collect data to show you personalized ads based on your online behavior.

ETHICAL AND LEGAL CONSIDERATIONS IN CYBERSECURITY

To protect your privacy, it's crucial to understand the value of your personal data and be aware of the ways it can be collected and used without your consent. Remember, you are not just a commodity to be bought and sold.

The Creepy World of Data Collection: The Big Brother is Watching

Data collection is an integral part of the digital ecosystem. Companies and organizations collect your data through various means, such as cookies, website tracking, social media platforms, and online surveys. They use this data to analyze consumer behavior, predict trends, and target specific audiences.

While data collection can provide benefits, it also poses significant risks to your privacy. It's essential to be aware of the ways your data is being collected and take steps to protect yourself. A few tips to keep in mind:

- Review privacy policies: Before using any online service or platform, take the time to read their privacy policy. Understand what data they collect, how they use it, and whether they share it with third parties.

- Opt-out of targeted advertising: Many companies allow you to opt-out of personalized ads. Take advantage of this option to reduce the amount of targeted advertising you see and limit the data collected about you.

- Use privacy-oriented search engines: Consider using search engines that focus on user privacy, such as DuckDuckGo or Startpage. These search engines don't track your searches or store your personal information.

- Limit social media sharing: Be cautious about the information you share on social media. Avoid revealing sensitive personal details and regularly review your privacy settings to control who can access your posts and information.

By being proactive and informed about data collection practices, you can take the first steps towards protecting your privacy online.

Data Breaches: When Your Sh*t Hits the Fan

Data breaches are on the rise, and their impact can be devastating. In a data breach, hackers gain unauthorized access to a company's database and extract sensitive information, such as usernames, passwords, credit card details, and personal identification information.

When a data breach occurs, your personal information is exposed, and the consequences can be severe. Hackers can use your stolen data for identity theft, financial fraud, or even blackmail. It's therefore essential to take steps to mitigate the impact of a potential data breach:

- Use unique passwords: Never reuse passwords across different accounts. If one account is compromised, it puts all your other accounts at risk. Consider using a reliable password manager that can generate and store complex passwords for you.

- Enable two-factor authentication (2FA): 2FA adds an extra layer of security by requiring an additional verification step, such as a fingerprint scan or a unique code sent to your smartphone, in addition to your password. This makes it much harder for hackers to access your accounts, even if they have your password.

- Regularly monitor your accounts: Keep an eye on your financial and online accounts for any suspicious activities. If you notice anything unusual, report it immediately to the respective companies and take steps to secure your account.

- Stay informed: Follow news updates about data breaches and take appropriate action if a company you have an account with experiences a breach. Often, companies offer free credit monitoring or identity theft protection services to affected individuals.

Remember, even with precautionary measures, data breaches can still happen. However, by implementing the above strategies, you can minimize the potential damage and protect yourself from the fallout.

Data Privacy Laws: Demanding Accountability from Big Tech

Governments around the world have recognized the importance of data privacy and have enacted laws and regulations to protect individuals. For example, the European Union implemented the General Data Protection Regulation (GDPR), which provides individuals with greater control over their personal data and imposes heavy fines on companies for non-compliance.

It is crucial to familiarize yourself with the data privacy laws in your country, as they form the backbone of your rights and protections online. Some key provisions you should be aware of include:

- Right to access: You have the right to request access to your personal data that companies collect and store. They must provide you with a copy of the data and information on how it is being used.

- Right to erasure: Also known as the "right to be forgotten," this gives you the ability to request the deletion of your personal data from a company's records.
- Consent requirements: Companies must obtain your explicit consent before collecting and using your personal data. They must provide clear and easily understandable information on how your data will be used.
- Data breach notifications: Companies are obligated to inform you in a timely manner if a data breach occurs that may put your personal data at risk.

By being aware of your rights and holding companies accountable, you can exercise greater control over your personal data and demand better privacy practices.

Protecting Your Online Reputation: Being a Responsible Digital Citizen

In the digital age, your online reputation is just as important as your offline reputation. Your actions, opinions, and online behavior can have lasting consequences. Therefore, it's vital to be a responsible digital citizen and take steps to protect and manage your online reputation.

Follow these guidelines to safeguard your online reputation:

- Think before you post: Before sharing anything online, pause and consider the potential impact. Remember that once something is shared, it can be challenging to remove it completely. Avoid posting content that could be seen as offensive, defamatory, or discriminatory.
- Monitor your digital footprint: Regularly search for your name online to see what information is associated with you. This will help you identify any negative or false information that may affect your reputation. If you find something harmful, take steps to address it.
- Set privacy settings: Manage your privacy settings on social media platforms to control who can see your posts and information. Be cautious about accepting friend requests or connections from people you don't know personally.
- Use a professional email address: When applying for jobs or engaging in professional activities, use a professional email address rather than a personal one. This creates a more polished and credible image.

Remember, maintaining a positive online reputation is essential for personal and professional success in the digital world.

Doxing Attacks: When Cybercriminals Target You

Doxing is a malicious practice where attackers gather and publish someone's personal information online without their consent. This information can include home addresses, phone numbers, email addresses, and even family details. Doxing attacks can lead to harassment, stalking, or even physical harm.

Protecting yourself from doxing attacks requires a combination of preventative measures and immediate action if you become a victim:

- Limit personal information online: Be mindful of the personal information you share online. Avoid posting details such as your full address, phone number, or other sensitive information that can be used against you.

- Strengthen your online accounts: Use strong, unique passwords for all your accounts and enable two-factor authentication whenever possible. Be cautious about the information you provide in account recovery options, like security questions, as this information can be used to bypass security measures.

- Monitor your online presence: Regularly conduct searches to see if any personal information associated with you is publicly available. If you find any of your details exposed, contact the website administrators and request them to remove the information.

- Report incidents: If you become a victim of doxing, report the incident to the appropriate authorities, such as your local law enforcement or cybercrime units. They can take action to track down the perpetrators and ensure your safety.

By being vigilant and proactive, you can reduce the risk of becoming a target of doxing attacks and protect your personal information from falling into the wrong hands.

Conclusion

Protecting your privacy rights in the digital age requires vigilance, awareness, and active participation in managing your digital presence. By understanding data privacy, staying informed about data collection practices and data breaches, demanding accountability from big tech, and being a responsible digital citizen, you can maintain control over your personal information and decrease the risk of getting f*cked over.

Remember, privacy is a fundamental right, and it's up to you to stand up for it in the face of a digital landscape filled with data predators. So, take control of your privacy, protect your digital shit, and navigate the wild west of the internet with confidence. You got this, Gen-Z!

Securing Your Fortress: Building Strong Defenses

Creating a Cybersecurity Mindset

Developing a Healthy Paranoia for Online Safety

In this section, we will talk about developing a healthy paranoia for online safety. It may sound a bit extreme, but with the growing threats in the cyber world, it's crucial to be on your toes and protect yourself from digital predators. So, let's dive into the world of online safety and learn how to develop a healthy level of paranoia.

Understanding the Nature of Online Threats

Before we can develop a healthy paranoia for online safety, it's important to understand the nature of online threats. In today's digital age, hackers, scammers, and other cybercriminals are constantly lurking in the shadows, waiting to pounce on unsuspecting internet users.

These threats come in various forms, ranging from phishing emails and malicious websites to ransomware attacks and identity theft. It's essential to be aware of these threats and understand the potential consequences they can have on your digital life.

The Power of Skepticism

One of the key elements in developing a healthy paranoia for online safety is skepticism. Don't believe everything you see or read online. Cybercriminals are masters of deception, using social engineering tactics to manipulate and trick their victims.

Always question the legitimacy of emails, messages, and websites. If something seems too good to be true or raises red flags, trust your instincts. Avoid clicking on suspicious links or downloading attachments from unknown sources. Remember, it's better to be safe than sorry.

Taking Responsibility for Your Digital Footprint

In today's interconnected world, protecting your online presence is crucial. Your digital footprint, consisting of the information you share on social media, websites, and other online platforms, can be a goldmine for cybercriminals.

Develop a healthy paranoia by taking responsibility for your digital footprint. Be mindful of the information you share online, especially personal and sensitive details. Adjust your privacy settings on social media platforms to restrict access to your information.

Additionally, be cautious when posting about your daily activities. Sharing too much information can make you an easy target for physical as well as digital threats. Remember, your digital presence can have real-life consequences.

Securing Your Digital Assets

In the digital wild west, you must fortify your digital assets to protect them from cybercriminals. Start by securing your devices with strong passwords and biometric authentication if available. Use a password manager to create unique and complex passwords for your online accounts.

Enable two-factor authentication (2FA) whenever possible. This adds an extra layer of security by requiring you to provide a second form of verification, such as a fingerprint or a unique code sent to your phone.

Furthermore, keep your devices and software up to date with the latest security patches. Cybercriminals often exploit vulnerabilities in outdated software to gain unauthorized access to your devices.

Educate Yourself about Common Cyber Threats

Knowledge is power when it comes to online safety. Educate yourself about common cyber threats and stay informed about the latest tactics used by cybercriminals. This will help you recognize and avoid potential dangers.

Stay up to date with news and resources provided by reputable cybersecurity organizations. They often share insights and tips on how to protect yourself from emerging threats.

CREATING A CYBERSECURITY MINDSET 45

Practice Cyber Hygiene

Just like maintaining personal hygiene to stay healthy, practicing cyber hygiene is essential to stay safe in the digital world. Regularly backup your important files to an external hard drive or a cloud storage service. This ensures that if you become a victim of a cyber-attack, your data remains safely stored.

Be cautious while using open Wi-Fi networks in public places. Avoid accessing sensitive information, such as online banking or email accounts, on unsecured networks. Use a virtual private network (VPN) to encrypt your internet traffic and protect your online activities from prying eyes.

Exercises and Tricks

To develop a healthy paranoia for online safety, here are a few exercises and tricks you can try:

- Practice phishing awareness: Familiarize yourself with common phishing tactics by using a phishing simulator that sends you mock phishing emails. Learn to identify the signs of a phishing email and avoid falling for the bait.

- Conduct a privacy check-up: Regularly review your privacy settings on social media platforms and other online accounts. Make sure you are only sharing information with the intended audience and adjust your settings accordingly.

- Challenge yourself to use stronger passwords: Set a goal to create unique and complex passwords for each of your online accounts. Use a password manager to generate and store these passwords securely.

Conclusion

Developing a healthy paranoia for online safety is not about being paranoid all the time. It's about being aware of the potential risks and taking proactive steps to protect yourself. By understanding the nature of online threats, practicing skepticism, and securing your digital assets, you can navigate the digital wild west with confidence. Stay informed, stay vigilant, and always remember that your digital safety is in your hands.

Now that we have covered the importance of developing a healthy paranoia for online safety, let's move on to another essential aspect of cybersecurity: passwords. In the next section, we will dive deep into the world of passwords and learn how to create strong and unique ones. Stay tuned, and don't be a dumbass with your passwords.

Recognizing Common Attack Vectors: Don't Be a Dumbass

In this section, we will dive into the world of common attack vectors in cybersecurity. Understanding these attack vectors is crucial for protecting yourself and your digital shit from the exploits of malicious hackers. So, let's get ready to arm ourselves with knowledge and not be dumbasses!

Phishing: The Art of the Deceptive Email

One of the most prevalent attack vectors used by cybercriminals is phishing. Phishing attacks involve sending deceptive emails that mimic legitimate messages from trusted organizations, with the goal of tricking recipients into revealing sensitive information or clicking on malicious links.

The dumbass can easily fall prey to a well-crafted phishing email. But fear not, we've got your back with some tips:

- **Beware of suspicious senders**: Check the email address of the sender. If it looks fishy (pun intended), don't click any links or provide any personal information.

- **Think twice before clicking**: Hover your mouse over any links in the email to see where they actually lead. If the URL looks sketchy or doesn't match the organization it claims to be from, don't click on it.

- **Take a closer look**: Spelling and grammar mistakes are red flags. Legitimate organizations usually put effort into their communication, while dumbasses... well, let's just say they don't.

- **Avoid sharing sensitive info**: Reputable organizations rarely ask for sensitive information via email. If you receive an email asking for passwords or credit card details, consider it a bright neon sign that says "Dumbass alert!"

So remember, don't be a dumbass. Stay vigilant and question everything when it comes to suspicious emails.

Social Engineering: Manipulating Human Sh*theads

Cybercriminals often prey on the weakest link in the cybersecurity chain: humans. Social engineering involves manipulating individuals to gain unauthorized access or divulge confidential information. These sh*theads take advantage of our trust, fear, or curiosity to get what they want.

Here are some common social engineering tactics to watch out for:

CREATING A CYBERSECURITY MINDSET

- **Phony phone calls:** Scammers may impersonate technical support personnel, bank employees, or government officials over the phone. They'll try to extract personal information or even convince you to install malicious software.

- **Pretexting:** These clever manipulators create fictional stories or scenarios to trick you into sharing sensitive information or granting access to restricted areas.

- **Baiting:** Remember the saying, "Curiosity killed the cat"? Well, it can also screw over a dumbass. Baiting involves enticing victims with an alluring offer, like a free movie download or a USB drive filled with "important files," which is, in reality, infected with malware.

- **Tailgating:** No, we're not talking about the person following you too closely in traffic. In the cybersecurity world, tailgating refers to someone physically following you through doors or checkpoints to gain unauthorized access to restricted areas.

To avoid falling into the trap of these social engineering tactics:

- **Verify the source:** Don't give out sensitive information over the phone unless you initiate the call and are certain of the recipient's identity.

- **Question everything:** If someone is asking for information or access, verify their credentials and validate their request. Don't be afraid to double-check with a supervisor or authority figure.

- **Keep your guard up:** Be skeptical of unexpected offers or requests that seem too good to be true. And remember, dumbasses don't get free movie downloads.

- **Secure your physical space:** Keep your doors locked and don't let random people tailgate you. If someone looks suspicious, be like a ninja and report their dastardly deeds.

By being aware of these social engineering techniques and practicing healthy skepticism, you can avoid being a dumbass and keep those cybercriminals at bay.

Malware: Beware of Digital Parasites

Malware, short for malicious software, is like the herpes of the digital world. It infects your devices, steals your data, and slows down your system. Common types of malware include viruses, worms, Trojans, ransomware, and spyware.

To prevent malware from turning you into a dumbass, take the following precautions:

- **Update thy software:** Keep your operating system, apps, and antivirus software up to date. Software updates often patch vulnerabilities that malware exploits.

- **Beware of sketchy downloads:** Don't download or install software from untrusted sources. Stick to reputable app stores or official websites, and read reviews before hitting that download button.

- **Don't be a clicker:** Avoid clicking on suspicious links or pop-up ads. If something feels fishy (and not in a good way), just don't click on it! Simple as that, dumbass.

- **Arm thy digital shields:** Install a reliable antivirus program and keep it updated. It's like having a badass cyber warrior defending your digital fortress.

- **Backup the sh*t out of your data:** Regularly backup your important files and store them in a secure location. This way, even if you encounter malware, you can give the middle finger to cybercriminals and restore your data.

By following these guidelines, you can protect yourself and avoid becoming a dumbass victim of malware.

Man-in-the-Middle Attacks: Not Your Average Threesome

Man-in-the-middle (MITM) attacks are like unwanted participants in a threesome—they intercept and alter communication between two parties without their knowledge. Cybercriminals position themselves between a victim's device and the intended recipient, eavesdropping on the conversation or even manipulating the data exchanged.

To avoid being a clueless dumbass in this kind of attack:

CREATING A CYBERSECURITY MINDSET

- **Use encrypted connections:** Whenever possible, opt for websites that use HTTPS encryption. This ensures that the communication between your device and the server is secure and makes it harder for a man-in-the-middle to snoop on your conversations.

- **Beware of public Wi-Fi:** Using public Wi-Fi networks can be risky. These networks are often targeted by cybercriminals to perform MITM attacks. So, be cautious when connecting to public Wi-Fi and avoid transmitting sensitive information.

- **Verify certificates:** When visiting websites, check if the SSL certificate is valid. If you get any warnings or errors, it's like a neon sign flashing, warning you not to be a dumbass.

- **Use a VPN:** A virtual private network (VPN) encrypts your internet connection and prevents eavesdroppers from intercepting your data. It's like wearing an invisibility cloak and giving a big middle finger to the man-in-the-middle.

- **Stay away from suspicious links:** If you receive a link from an unknown source or via unsecured channels, don't click on it. Play it safe and only interact with links from trusted sources.

By taking these precautions, you can avoid being the unsuspecting fool in a man-in-the-middle attack and keep your digital conversations private and secure.

Conclusion: Stay Woke, Stay Safe

Congratulations on making it through this section without being a dumbass! You've learned about common attack vectors in the wild west of cyberspace and how to safeguard yourself against them.

Remember, cybersecurity is a continuously evolving field, and cybercriminals will always come up with new tricks. So, stay woke, educate yourself, and adapt to the changing threat landscape.

In the next section, we'll delve into the world of passwords and how to choose stronger ones than "Password123." Get ready to level up your cybersecurity game, you badass!

Cultivating Critical Thinking Skills to Identify Bullsh*t

In the digital age, where information is just a click away, it's critical to develop robust critical thinking skills to separate the valuable nuggets of truth from the steaming piles of bullsh*t that pollute the online world. In this section, we'll explore some strategies and techniques to cultivate these skills and avoid falling prey to misinformation, deception, and manipulation.

Understanding the Importance of Critical Thinking

Critical thinking is like a superpower in the digital wild west. It allows you to analyze and evaluate information, discern fact from fiction, and make well-informed decisions. In a world where fake news, misinformation campaigns, and online scams abound, critical thinking is your armor against the bullsh*t that's out there.

Question Everything

The first step in cultivating critical thinking skills is to question everything. Don't accept information at face value just because it aligns with your preconceived notions or beliefs. Challenge assumptions, demand evidence, and scrutinize the sources of information. Remember, just because something is trending or being shared by millions doesn't mean it's true. Truth doesn't care about popularity.

Verify Your Sources

In the age of Photoshop and deepfakes, it's essential to verify the credibility of your sources. Not all websites, news articles, or social media posts are created equal. Look for reputable sources, such as established news organizations, academic institutions, or government websites. Cross-reference information from multiple sources to ensure consistency and accuracy. Be mindful of bias and hidden agendas that can skew the narrative.

Spotting Logical Fallacies

Logical fallacies are like the footprints of bullsh*t. They are flawed arguments that manipulate emotions or exploit cognitive biases to deceive or mislead. By familiarizing yourself with common logical fallacies, you can identify and call out the bullsh*t when you see it. Some examples include ad hominem attacks, false dichotomies, strawman arguments, and appeals to authority. Let's break down a couple of these fallacies:

- Ad Hominem: This fallacy attacks the person making the argument instead of addressing the argument itself. For example, dismissing someone's opinion because they belong to a certain political party or have a particular background.

- False Dichotomy: This fallacy presents a situation as an either/or choice when, in reality, there are more options. It's a tactic often used to oversimplify complex issues. For instance, claiming that you're either with us or against us, leaving no room for nuanced discourse.

Being aware of these fallacies will help you cut through the bullsh*t and focus on the actual substance of an argument.

Develop Critical Reading Skills

In a sea of text, developing critical reading skills is crucial. When faced with an article, blog post, or even a social media caption, don't just skim through it like a brain-dead zombie. Read actively and attentively. Analyze the author's tone, language, and writing style. Look for supporting evidence and logical consistency. Pay attention to any biases or manipulation techniques being employed. This will enable you to separate well-reasoned arguments from unfounded claims and bullsh*t.

Embrace Skepticism, but Stay Open

Being skeptical is important, but it's equally important to approach information with an open mind. Don't fall into the trap of being so skeptical that you reject everything outright. Stay receptive to new ideas and evidence, while still subjecting them to critical scrutiny. The goal is not to be closed-minded but to strike a balance between skepticism and intellectual curiosity.

Practice Critical Thinking in Everyday Life

Critical thinking is not just an academic exercise - it's a mindset that should be applied to every aspect of your life. Use it to evaluate the claims made by advertisers, politicians, and even your friends and family. Apply it when making important decisions, such as choosing a career path or investing your hard-earned cash. By practicing critical thinking regularly, you'll hone your skills and become a master at identifying bullsh*t.

Be Aware of Your Own Biases

Lastly, self-awareness is a crucial aspect of critical thinking. Recognize that we all have biases that can cloud our judgment. These biases can come from our experiences, cultural upbringing, or the echo chambers of social media. Be mindful of your own biases and actively seek out diverse perspectives. Challenge your assumptions and be open to changing your opinion based on new evidence.

Unconventional Tip: The Bullsh*t Detection Kit

To help you navigate the treacherous waters of bullsh*t, we present to you the Bullsh*t Detection Kit – a handy toolkit of questions to ask when confronted with suspicious or dubious information:

- Who is the source of the information, and are they credible?
- What evidence supports the claims being made?
- Are there alternative explanations or perspectives?
- Does the argument rely on logical fallacies or emotional manipulation?
- Are there any conflicts of interest or hidden agendas?

By using this kit, you'll be well-equipped to spot bullsh*t from a mile away!

Summary

In this section, we explored the importance of cultivating critical thinking skills to identify bullsh*t in the digital landscape. We discussed the need to question everything, verify sources, spot logical fallacies, develop critical reading skills, and embrace skepticism while staying open-minded. We also emphasized the significance of practicing critical thinking in everyday life and being aware of our own biases. Remember, in the digital wild west, only those armed with critical thinking skills can navigate the bullsh*t-filled terrain unscathed.

Now, it's time to put your critical thinking skills to the test with some exercises.

Exercises

1. Find an article online and analyze it using the Bullsh*t Detection Kit. Identify any logical fallacies, biases, or questionable sources.

2. Choose a controversial topic and research it from different perspectives. Write a short essay presenting all sides of the argument and supporting your analysis with credible sources.

3. Imagine you come across a social media post making sweeping claims about a product's miraculous health benefits. Using critical thinking, analyze the post and develop a list of probing questions to challenge the claims made.

Resources:

- "Thinking, Fast and Slow" by Daniel Kahneman: This book explores the two systems of thinking - fast and intuitive vs. slow and deliberate - and helps you understand the shortcuts and biases that influence your decision-making.

- www.snopes.com: A fact-checking website that debunks urban legends, hoaxes, and misinformation.

- www.pewresearch.org: A reputable source for unbiased research and polling data on a wide range of topics.

Remember, becoming a critical thinker is an ongoing journey. So, keep honing your skills, stay vigilant, and never stop questioning the bullsh*t that comes your way.

Further Reading

- "The Skeptic's Guide to the Universe: How to Know What's Really Real in a World Increasingly Full of Fake" by Steven Novella et al.
- "A Field Guide to Lies: Critical Thinking in the Information Age" by Daniel J. Levitin.
- "Factfulness: Ten Reasons We're Wrong About the World - And Why Things Are Better Than You Think" by Hans Rosling et al.

Being a Responsible Digital Citizen: Don't Be a Troll

In this section, we'll dive into the importance of being a responsible digital citizen and avoiding troll-like behaviors online. With the rise of social media and an increasing amount of time spent online, it's vital to understand the impact our words and actions can have on others. Let's explore some key principles and guidelines to help you navigate the digital world with respect and decency.

Understanding the Power of Words

Words have always been powerful, but in the digital age, their impact is magnified. When communicating online, it's easy to detach ourselves from the consequences of our words. This has led to a culture of trolling, where individuals intentionally provoke and harass others for personal amusement. Being a responsible digital citizen means recognizing the power our words hold and using them to build a positive online community.

Promoting Respect and Empathy

Responsible digital citizenship starts with promoting respect and empathy towards others. The internet is a diverse space, bringing together people from different backgrounds, cultures, and beliefs. Understanding and appreciating this diversity is crucial in creating an inclusive online environment. Treat others with kindness, respect their opinions even if you disagree, and refrain from engaging in personal attacks or cyberbullying.

Constructive Communication

One of the hallmarks of being a responsible digital citizen is engaging in constructive communication. Rather than seeking conflict or trying to "win" arguments, focus on fostering meaningful discussions. Ask questions, seek to understand different perspectives, and respond with thoughtful and well-reasoned arguments. Remember that the goal should be to find common ground and learn from one another, rather than tearing each other down.

Fact-Checking and Critical Thinking

The internet is a breeding ground for misinformation, and it's all too easy to fall into the trap of sharing false or misleading information without thinking twice. As a responsible digital citizen, it's crucial to fact-check information before sharing it. Develop critical thinking skills to evaluate the credibility of sources and question the validity of claims. By doing so, you can help combat the spread of misinformation and contribute to a more informed online community.

Taking Responsibility for Your Actions

Digital anonymity can sometimes lead to a sense of detachment from real-world consequences. However, it's important to remember that our actions online can have real-life impacts. Being a responsible digital citizen means taking accountability for your words and actions. Think before you post, consider how your words may affect others, and be ready to apologize if you make a mistake. Taking responsibility for your online behavior is a vital part of promoting a healthy and respectful digital community.

The Power of Context and Tone

Online interactions lack the subtleties of face-to-face communication, such as body language and tone of voice. As a result, messages can easily be misinterpreted or taken out of context. When engaging with others online, be mindful of the words you use and how they may be perceived. Avoid sarcasm or jokes that could be seen as hurtful, and when in doubt, provide additional context to ensure your intentions are clear.

Resisting the Urge to Engage in Troll-like Behavior

Troll-like behavior, characterized by intentionally inflammatory or disruptive actions, has become an unfortunate norm in many online spaces. As a responsible digital citizen, it's essential to resist the urge to engage in such behavior. Instead, focus on promoting positivity and contributing to a healthy online environment. Don't feed the trolls by responding to their provocations, and report or block individuals who consistently engage in abusive or disruptive behavior.

Resources for Responsible Digital Citizenship

To further enhance your understanding of responsible digital citizenship, there are various resources available for you to explore:

- "The Art of Digital Etiquette" by Karen Freberg: This book provides valuable insights into online communication and the importance of responsible digital behavior.
- Common Sense Media (www.commonsensemedia.org): A website offering resources, tips, and advice for parents, educators, and students on navigating the digital world responsibly.
- Digital Citizenship Education (www.digitalcitizenship.net): An online platform dedicated to promoting responsible digital citizenship through educational resources and curriculum ideas.

Exercise: Reflecting on Your Digital Behavior

Take a moment to reflect on your digital behavior and consider the following questions:

1. Have you ever engaged in troll-like behavior online? If so, why did you do it, and what were the consequences?

2. How can you promote respect and empathy in your online interactions?

3. What steps can you take to ensure the information you share is accurate and reliable?

4. Have you witnessed or experienced cyberbullying? How did it make you feel, and what could have been done to prevent it?

5. How can you contribute to a positive and inclusive online community?

By honestly answering these questions and reflecting on your digital behavior, you can make positive changes and become a more responsible digital citizen.

Summary

Being a responsible digital citizen requires us to recognize the power of our online words, promote respect and empathy, engage in constructive communication, fact-check and think critically, take responsibility for our actions, consider context and tone, resist troll-like behavior, and seek out resources for further learning. By embodying these principles, we can contribute to a safer, more inclusive, and respectful digital world. So, be a responsible digital citizen, and don't be a troll!

Passwords: The Gatekeepers of Your Digital Shit

Choosing Strong and Unique Passwords: No More "Password123"

In this section, we'll dive into the importance of choosing strong and unique passwords to protect your digital shit. Let's face it, using "Password123" as your password is about as secure as leaving your front door wide open in a crime-ridden neighborhood.

The Weakness of Common Passwords

Before we delve into the art of creating strong passwords, let's take a moment to understand why common passwords are as effective as a wet paper bag in a hurricane. Hackers and cybercriminals have become increasingly sophisticated and can easily crack weak passwords using brute-force attacks, dictionary attacks, or by exploiting common patterns.

Imagine you're the proud owner of a brand new smartphone, equipped with state-of-the-art security features, but you decide to use the password "123456" to protect it. Well, congratulations, you might as well leave your phone lying on a park bench with a sticky note attached saying, "Help yourself!"

Common passwords, such as "password," "qwerty," or "123456," are like low-hanging fruits for hackers. They can easily guess or crack these passwords using automated tools in a matter of seconds. And trust me, hackers have nothing better to do than to make you their next target.

The Anatomy of a Strong Password

Now that you understand the perils of using weak passwords, let's talk about what makes a password strong and secure. A strong password is like a fortress - it should be complex, unpredictable, and unique to each account you have. Here are some characteristics of a strong password:

- **Length:** The longer, the better. Aim for a minimum of 12 characters.

- **Complexity:** Mix it up! Use a combination of uppercase and lowercase letters, numbers, and special characters.

- **Unpredictability:** Avoid using common words, phrases, or personal information that can be easily guessed.

- **Uniqueness:** Each online account should have its own unique password.

Now, I know what you're thinking: "How the hell am I supposed to remember all these random ass passwords?" Well, fear not, my friend. We'll dive into password management tools and best practices later on, but for now, let's focus on creating strong passwords.

Creating Strong Passwords That You Can Remember

Creating a strong password doesn't mean you have to sacrifice your sanity trying to remember it. Here are some practical strategies to create strong passwords that are easy for you to remember:

- **Passphrases:** Instead of using a single word as your password, consider using a passphrase. For example, "I love eating tacos at 2AM!" is a strong and memorable password.

- **Substitutions:** Replace letters with similar-looking characters or numbers. For example, you can replace "o" with "0" or "l" with "1" to make your password more complex.

- **Personalization:** Add a personal touch to your password by incorporating something meaningful to you. For example, "ILoveMyDog_Max" is a strong password for a dog lover.

- **Song Lyrics or Quotes:** Use a line from your favorite song or a memorable quote as a password. Just make sure it's not something easily guessable or publicly known.

Remember, the goal is to create a password that is difficult for others to crack but easy for you to remember. Take your time, get creative, and come up with unique passwords for each of your accounts.

Testing the Strength of Your Password

So, you've crafted what you think is a strong password. But how do you know for sure? Well, it's time to put it to the test with some password strength-checking tools.

There are numerous online tools and websites that can evaluate the strength of your password. These tools analyze factors such as the length, complexity, and predictability of your password to determine its strength. They can also offer suggestions on how to improve your password if it's considered weak.

Here are a few popular password strength-checking tools you can try out:

- **How Secure Is My Password?** - A simple and straightforward website that estimates how long it would take for a computer to crack your password.

- **Password Meter** - A tool that provides a strength score and feedback on how to improve your password.

- **Have I Been Pwned?** - A website that checks if your password has been exposed in any known data breaches. Remember, even the strongest password won't save you if the website you use it on has been compromised.

Use these tools to assess the strength of your passwords and make any necessary adjustments if they are deemed weak. Your digital security is in your hands, so take the time to ensure your passwords are up to par.

Protecting your Passwords

Now that you have strong and unique passwords, it's crucial to protect them from prying eyes. Here are a few best practices to keep your passwords safe:

PASSWORDS: THE GATEKEEPERS OF YOUR DIGITAL SHIT

- **Never share your passwords:** Treat your passwords like your toothbrush - don't share them with anyone. Not your best friend, not your significant other, nobody.

- **Use a password manager:** Password managers are secure tools that store your passwords in an encrypted vault. They also have the functionality to generate and autofill strong passwords for you. Some popular password managers include LastPass, Dashlane, and 1Password.

- **Enable two-factor authentication (2FA):** 2FA adds an extra layer of security by requiring a second form of verification, such as a fingerprint scan or a unique code sent to your phone, in addition to your password.

- **Regularly update your passwords:** It's good practice to update your passwords periodically, especially for sensitive accounts like your email or online banking. Aim to change passwords every three to six months.

With these practices in place, you can rest assured that your passwords are as secure as a fortress.

Unconventional Tip: XKCD Passwords

If you're seeking a more unconventional approach to password creation, you might want to consider XKCD-style passwords. XKCD is a popular online comic that humorously conveys complex ideas. One of their comics famously suggests creating passwords using four common words as a memorable yet secure alternative.

For example, a password like "correct-horse-battery-staple" is not only strong but also easy to remember. The concept behind this approach is that using long, random words creates a passphrase that is difficult for hackers to crack but easy for you to recall.

While this method may not be suitable for all situations, it can be a fun and effective strategy for creating unique passwords.

Summary

In this section, we explored the importance of choosing strong and unique passwords. We discussed the weaknesses of common passwords, the characteristics of strong passwords, and practical strategies for creating and remembering them. We also highlighted the significance of testing the strength of your passwords and protecting them using best practices such as password managers and enabling two-factor authentication.

Remember, your password is the first line of defense in protecting your digital shit. Don't be lazy, get creative, and beef up your passwords. Your online security depends on it.

The Art of Password Management: Tools and Best Practices

In this section, we're going to explore the art of password management and equip you with the tools and best practices to create strong and secure passwords. We'll also discuss the importance of using password managers to simplify your life and keep your digital shit locked up tight. So let's dive in, my friends!

Why Passwords Matter

Before we get into the nitty-gritty of password management, let's talk about why passwords matter in the first place. In the digital age, passwords are like the keys to your online kingdom. They protect your personal information, financial data, and online accounts from falling into the wrong hands. If you want to safeguard your precious digital shit, you need to take passwords seriously.

Creating Strong and Unique Passwords

The first rule of password management is to create strong and unique passwords for each of your online accounts. I know, it's a pain in the ass to remember a gazillion passwords, but trust me, it's worth the effort. Here's how you can do it like a boss:

1. **Length Matters:** Long passwords are your friends. Aim for a minimum of 12-16 characters. The more, the merrier. Mix it up with uppercase and lowercase letters, numbers, and special characters. Don't be lazy and go for "password123" or "letmein". Hackers eat those crap for breakfast!

2. **Avoid Personal Info:** Please, for the love of all things sacred, do not use personal information in your passwords. That means no pet names, birthdates, or the name of your favorite 90s boy band. Hackers are smarter than that. And no, substituting "3" for "E" doesn't make it any safer. So be creative and leave your personal shit out of it.

3. **Avoid Dictionary Words:** Using dictionary words in your passwords is like handing a hacker the key to your digital kingdom. They can easily crack that shit with their fancy-ass algorithms. So steer clear of common words and get your creative juices flowing. Combine random words, throw in some numbers and symbols, and voila! You've got yourself a strong password, my friend.

4. **No Reusing:** I know it's tempting to reuse passwords for multiple accounts because, hey, who's got time for memorizing a gazillion passwords? But that's like using the same key for your car, house, and secret lair. If one of them gets hacked, your whole life is at risk. So, don't be a lazy dumbass and create unique passwords for each account.

5. **Don't Write 'Em Down:** Now, I already know what you're thinking. "But Herkimer, how the hell am I supposed to remember all these crazy-ass passwords?" Fear not, my friend, because we've got the perfect solution for you.

The Power of Password Managers

Enter password managers, the unsung heroes of cybersecurity. These bad boys are like your personal bouncers, guarding your passwords with military-grade encryption. They not only store and organize all your passwords in a secure vault but also generate strong and unique passwords for you. Here's why you should embrace password managers like your life depends on it:

1. **Convenience at Your Fingertips:** Password managers make your life easier by auto-filling your login credentials across different devices and web browsers. No more wasting time typing in passwords or hitting that annoying "Forgot Password" button. Just sit back, relax, and let your password manager do the work.

2. **Enhanced Security:** With password managers, you only need to remember one master password to access your vault. This means you can create an insanely complex master password that even the most badass hackers would struggle to crack. Oh, and did I mention that password managers also have a nifty feature called two-factor authentication? It's like adding an extra layer of armored protection to your digital fortress.

3. **Sync Across Devices:** Whether you're browsing the web on your laptop, tablet, or smartphone, password managers got your back. They sync your passwords seamlessly across all your devices, so you can access your accounts anytime, anywhere. Say goodbye to the days of pulling your hair out in frustration because you can't remember which password goes where.

4. **Password Generation Magic:** Tired of wracking your brain for strong and unique passwords? Let the password manager work its magic. It can generate

passwords that are damn near uncrackable. So say goodbye to "password123" and say hello to "fZq&7$yP!Mv2u"

Choosing the Right Password Manager

Now that you're convinced of the awesomeness of password managers, it's time to choose the right one for you. Here are a few things to consider:

- **Security Features:** Look for a password manager that uses strong encryption algorithms, like AES-256, to protect your data. It should also have two-factor authentication to keep your vault under lock and key.

- **User-Friendly Interface:** Ain't nobody got time for a clunky and confusing interface. Choose a password manager with a sleek and intuitive design that makes your life easier, not harder.

- **Cross-Platform Compatibility:** Make sure the password manager works across all your devices and operating systems. It should play nice with your smartphone, laptop, tablet, and whatever funky gadgets you've got.

- **Customer Support:** In case shit hits the fan or you have questions, good customer support can save your digital ass. Look for password managers that have a responsive support team ready to assist you.

Best Practices for Password Management

Now that you've chosen your password manager, let's go over some best practices to ensure your passwords are as secure as Fort Knox:

- **Keep Your Master Password Safe:** Treat your master password like a top-secret government document. Don't write it down and store it in your underwear drawer. Commit it to memory or use a passphrase that's long, memorable, and totally badass.

- **Regularly Update Your Passwords:** Ain't nobody got time for stale passwords. Update your passwords regularly, especially for your most sensitive accounts. And please, for the love of all things sacred, don't reuse old passwords. That shit's just asking for trouble.

- **Enable Two-Factor Authentication:** Two-factor authentication is like adding an extra lock to your digital fortress. It provides an additional layer

PASSWORDS: THE GATEKEEPERS OF YOUR DIGITAL SHIT

of security by requiring a second form of authentication, such as a fingerprint scan or a unique code sent to your phone. So turn that shit on wherever possible.

- **Beware of Phishing Attacks:** No matter how strong your passwords are, they won't protect you from phishing attacks. So keep an eye out for suspicious emails, messages, or websites that try to trick you into revealing your login credentials. Stay skeptical, my friend.

- **Regularly Back Up Your Password Manager:** Just like you back up your important files, it's essential to back up your password manager. In case of a catastrophic failure or a lost device, having a backup will save you from a whole lot of headache and tears.

Unconventional Yet Relevant Tip: The Diceware Method

Okay, my friend, here's a little unconventional tip for you: the Diceware method. If you want to create a truly random and secure password without relying on a password manager, this method is for you. Here's how it works:

1. Roll a six-sided dice five times. Write down the numbers you roll each time.

2. Use those numbers to look up corresponding words from the Diceware word list. Each word represents one dice roll.

3. Keep rolling the dice and writing down the numbers until you have a password of desired length, let's say 6-8 words.

4. Congratulations! You've created a password that's cryptographically secure and nearly impossible for hackers to crack. You're a badass, my friend!

Conclusion

And there you have it, my Gen-Z comrades. You now possess the knowledge and power to create strong and unique passwords like a cybersecurity ninja. Remember to embrace password managers, follow best practices, and stay vigilant against those sneaky phishing attacks. With these tools and practices in your arsenal, your digital shit will be as secure as Fort Knox in the Wild West of cyberspace. So go forth and protect your digital kingdom, my friends!

Two-Factor Authentication: Adding an Extra Layer of Protection

In the wild west of the digital world, where cybercriminals are armed with sophisticated tools and cunning strategies, protecting your digital shit requires more than just a strong password. This is where two-factor authentication (2FA) steps in, offering an extra layer of protection to keep the bad guys at bay. In this section, we'll dive into the world of 2FA, exploring its principles, implementation methods, and why you should give a shit about it.

The Need for 2FA

You might be wondering, "Why the hell do I need 2FA? Isn't a strong password enough?" Well, dear reader, let me burst your bubble for a moment. While a strong password is certainly a good defense, it's not foolproof. Cybercriminals are constantly coming up with new ways to crack passwords, whether through brute force attacks or by using stolen password databases from data breaches.

2FA adds an extra layer of security by requiring you to provide two types of identification before granting access to your digital accounts. It's like having a secret handshake in addition to your password. Even if a hacker manages to crack your password, they'll still need the second factor to gain access.

How Does 2FA Work?

Alright, let's get down to the nitty-gritty of how this sh*t actually works. 2FA typically involves three components: something you know, something you have, and something you are. Let's break them down:

1. **Something You Know:** This is usually your password or a PIN. It's something that only you should know and is considered the first factor of authentication.

2. **Something You Have:** This can be a physical device like your smartphone or a hardware token. It generates a unique code that changes periodically, and you'll need to provide this code as the second factor.

3. **Something You Are:** This is the most badass factor of all. It involves biometrics like your fingerprint, face, or voice. Biometric authentication methods are becoming more common as smartphones integrate features like fingerprint scanners and facial recognition.

Now, let's see how these factors come together in practice.

Methods of 2FA

There are several methods to implement 2FA, each with its own pros and cons. Let's explore some of the most common ones:

1. **SMS-based 2FA:** When you enable this method, your service provider will send a unique code to your mobile phone via SMS. You'll then enter this code as the second factor during login. While convenient, this method has some security concerns. Hackers can intercept SMS messages or clone SIM cards to gain unauthorized access.

2. **Authentication Apps:** These handy apps generate time-based one-time passwords (TOTPs) that change every few seconds. Examples include Google Authenticator, Authy, and Microsoft Authenticator. These apps use the TOTP algorithm, which is based on a shared secret key between your device and the service you're authenticating with. To complete the 2FA process, you simply enter the current code displayed on the app.

3. **Hardware Tokens:** This method involves physical devices, like USB keys or smart cards, that generate one-time passwords or use cryptographic protocols to authenticate. Hardware tokens are more secure than SMS-based methods since they're not susceptible to SIM swapping or interception. However, they can be expensive and cumbersome to carry around.

4. **Biometric 2FA:** As mentioned earlier, biometrics like fingerprints, facial recognition, or voiceprints can be used as the second factor. You've probably encountered this on your smartphone, where you can unlock it using your fingerprint or face. While convenient, biometric data can be compromised or imitated, so it's not foolproof.

Advantages and Challenges of 2FA

Now that you have a good grasp of 2FA, let's take a moment to break down its advantages and challenges:

Advantages:

- *Increased Security:* 2FA provides an extra layer of protection, making it harder for attackers to gain unauthorized access to your accounts.

- *Mitigates Password Vulnerabilities:* Even if your password gets compromised, the second factor acts as a barrier to protect your accounts.

- *Flexible Implementation:* With a variety of methods available, you can choose the one that best suits your needs and preferences.

Challenges:

- *Usability and Convenience:* Some 2FA methods can be cumbersome or time-consuming. Striking the balance between security and usability is a challenge.

- *Dependency on External Factors:* Certain 2FA methods, like SMS-based authentication, require a stable network connection, which may not always be available.

- *Single Point of Failure:* If you lose access to the second factor or it gets compromised, you may face challenges recovering your account.

Tips for Using 2FA

Now that you're pumped about adding an extra layer of protection with 2FA, let's cover some tips to make your experience smooth and secure:

- *Enable 2FA Everywhere:* Whenever possible, enable 2FA on all your online accounts, including social media, email, and banking platforms. Don't leave any digital stone unturned!

- *Use Authentication Apps:* Authentication apps like Google Authenticator provide a more secure and convenient method compared to SMS-based authentication. Consider using them whenever available.

- *Backup Codes:* Many services offer backup codes that you can print or save in a secure location. These codes can be used as a backup if you can't access your second factor temporarily.

- *Biometrics with Caution:* While biometric authentication can be convenient, remember that your biometric data cannot be changed once compromised. Use it wisely and understand the potential risks involved.

- *Keep Your Second Factors Secure:* Treat your second factors, whether it's your smartphone or a hardware token, like precious gems. Keep them in a safe place and avoid sharing them with anyone.

Conclusion

Congratulations, partner! You've learned how to add an extra layer of protection to your digital fortress with 2FA. As cybercriminals continue to roam the wild west of the digital world, implementing 2FA is an essential step to safeguarding your digital shit. Remember to keep a good balance between security and convenience, and always stay ahead of the game by using the latest authentication methods. Now go out there and be the badass defender of your own cyber domain!

Yeehaw!

Dealing with Password Spraying and Credential Stuffing Attacks

In the chaotic world of cybersecurity, password spraying and credential stuffing attacks are two notorious techniques used by cybercriminals to gain unauthorized access to user accounts. In this section, we'll dive into the nitty-gritty of these attacks and explore effective countermeasures to safeguard your digital shit.

Understanding Password Spraying

Picture this: a cybercriminal stands on the digital frontier, armed with a massive list of common passwords like "password123" and "qwerty". With a single click, they unleash a storm of login attempts against a large number of user accounts, aiming to find the weakest link. This is the essence of a password spraying attack.

The goal of a password spraying attack is simple: to discover accounts with weak passwords that can be easily cracked. By targeting multiple accounts with a small number of common passwords, attackers aim to bypass account lockouts and evade detection. These attacks are often carried out in a slow and stealthy manner to fly under the radar of security systems.

Fighting Back: Defense Strategies

As a savvy digital citizen, you're not going to sit back and let the cybercriminals have their way with your accounts. Here are some badass defense strategies to level the playing field:

1. **Strong and Unique Passwords:** Duh. We've said it a million times, but it's worth repeating: use passwords that are long, complex, and unique for each of your accounts. Steer clear of easily guessable shit like your pet's name or your date of birth. Get creative and use a password manager to keep track of your login credentials.

2. **Account Lockouts and Rate Limiting:** Implement account lockouts and rate limiting mechanisms on your online accounts. This means that if someone

tries to guess your password multiple times within a short period, the account locks down or imposes a waiting period between login attempts. This makes life harder for password sprayers.

3. Multi-Factor Authentication (MFA): MFA is like adding extra locks to your digital fortress. By enabling MFA, you require an additional verification step, such as a one-time code sent to your phone, to access your account. Even if the password spraying attack succeeds, the attacker won't be able to get in without the second factor.

4. User Education: The weakest link in any cybersecurity defense is often the human element. Educate yourself and others about the risks of weak passwords and the importance of using strong ones. Spread the word on the digital battlefield and make sure your friends and family are fighting the good fight too.

The Menace of Credential Stuffing

Password spraying is just one side of the coin. Now, let's shine a light on the menace known as credential stuffing. Brace yourself, because shit's about to get real.

In a credential stuffing attack, the cybercriminal takes stolen or leaked username and password combinations from one platform and tries them out on multiple other platforms. They exploit the fact that many people reuse their passwords across different accounts, hoping to strike gold with the same credentials.

Protecting Yourself: A Battle Plan

Credential stuffing attacks are a major pain in the ass, but there are ways to protect yourself and avoid becoming a victim:

1. Unique Passwords (Again): Seriously, don't reuse passwords. It may seem like a hassle, but trust us, it's worth it. Create unique passwords for each online account, no matter how insignificant it may seem. That way, even if one account gets compromised, the rest will remain secure.

2. Regularly Monitor Breach Reports: Stay vigilant and keep an eye on breach reports and news about data leaks. If a platform you use has had a security breach, change your password immediately. And remember, change it to something strong and unique!

3. Use a Password Manager: We've mentioned password managers before, but they deserve another shout-out. Password managers generate and store unique passwords for each of your online accounts, making it a breeze to follow the "unique passwords" rule. Plus, they often offer features like breach alerts that notify you if your login credentials are compromised.

4. **Implement CAPTCHA or Similar Technologies:** CAPTCHA, those annoying tests that ask you to prove you're not a robot, can actually be your ally in the fight against credential stuffing attacks. By adding CAPTCHA or similar technologies to your login pages, you can complicate the automated login attempts of cybercriminals.

Putting Your Knowledge into Action

Now that you're equipped with a kickass arsenal of knowledge about password spraying and credential stuffing attacks, it's time to put it into action. Here are a couple of exercises to test your skills:

Exercise 1: Imagine you're tasked with securing an online platform that has been experiencing a surge in password spraying attacks. Develop a plan to defend against such attacks, considering both technical and user-focused measures.

Exercise 2: Conduct an audit of your own online accounts and determine if any of your passwords have been compromised in previous data breaches. Take necessary actions to secure your accounts and protect your digital shit.

Resources and Further Reading

To continue your journey into the wild west of password security, check out the following resources:

- Book: "Perfect Passwords: Selection, Protection, Authentication" by Man Young Rhee

- Website: "Have I Been Pwned" (https://haveibeenpwned.com/)

- Website: OWASP (Open Web Application Security Project) "Password Storage Cheat Sheet" (https://owasp.org/www-project-cheat-sheets/cheatsheets/Password_Storage_Che

Remember, in the digital wild west, strong passwords and smart practices are your weapons of choice against password spraying and credential stuffing attacks. Stay vigilant, stay informed, and protect your digital shit like a badass cyber gunslinger!

Protecting Your Devices and Networks

Securing Your Smartphone: More Than Just a Tinder Machine

In this section, we will explore the various steps you can take to secure your smartphone and protect it from malicious attacks. Your smartphone is not just a device for swiping left or right on Tinder; it contains a treasure trove of personal information that can be exploited by hackers if not properly protected. So, let's dive in and learn how to fortify your smartphone against cyber threats.

Understanding the Risks

Before we jump into the measures you can take to secure your smartphone, it's important to understand the potential risks you face in the digital Wild West. Here are some common threats:

- **Malware:** These are malicious software programs that can infect your smartphone, steal your personal information, or even take control of your device.

- **Phishing:** This is when attackers use deceitful tactics, such as fake emails or websites, to trick you into revealing sensitive information like passwords or credit card details.

- **Data Theft:** Hackers are always on the prowl for personal data stored on smartphones, such as contacts, messages, and photos. This data can be exploited for identity theft or sold on the dark web.

- **Unauthorized Access:** If someone gains physical access to your smartphone, they can potentially unlock it, extract your data, or plant malware.

Now that we understand the risks, let's move on to the steps you can take to secure your smartphone.

Update Your Software

First things first, ensure that your smartphone's operating system (OS) and apps are up to date. Software updates often include patches to fix security vulnerabilities, so it's crucial to stay current. Enable automatic updates whenever possible so that you don't miss out on crucial security fixes.

Lock Down Your Device

One of the simplest yet most effective ways to secure your smartphone is by using a strong passcode or biometric authentication. Here's what you can do:

- **Use a strong passcode:** Avoid predictable passcodes like "1234" or "password." Instead, opt for a longer and more complex passcode that includes a combination of numbers, letters, and special characters.

- **Biometric authentication:** Many smartphones now feature biometric security options like fingerprint scanners or facial recognition. Enable these features for an added layer of protection.

- Enable a **remote wipe:** In case your smartphone gets lost or stolen, having a remote wipe feature allows you to erase all the data on your device remotely. This way, you can ensure that your personal information doesn't fall into the wrong hands.

Install a Reliable Security App

Just like computers, smartphones can benefit from antivirus and security apps. Look for reputable security apps in your device's app store and install one that offers features such as:

- **Malware scanning:** Scan your smartphone for malware regularly to detect and remove any malicious software.

- **Safe web browsing:** Some security apps offer safe browsing features that warn you about potentially harmful websites or block malicious links.

- **Anti-theft features:** Look for apps that have anti-theft features such as remote locking, tracking, or data wiping to protect your smartphone in case of loss or theft.

Remember to keep your security app up to date and perform regular scans to ensure your smartphone remains protected.

Be Mindful of App Permissions

When installing apps on your smartphone, it's important to pay attention to the permissions they request. Some apps may ask for unnecessary access to your personal data, which can pose a privacy risk. Here's what you can do:

- **Read the permissions:** Before installing an app, carefully review the permissions it requests. If an app requests access to sensitive information that seems unrelated to its functionality, consider whether it's worth the risk.

- **Manage permissions:** Most smartphones allow you to manage app permissions individually. Limit the access granted to apps by disabling unnecessary permissions in your device settings.

Use Caution with Public Wi-Fi

Public Wi-Fi networks can be convenient, but they also pose security risks. Avoid transmitting sensitive data or accessing personal accounts when connected to public Wi-Fi. If you must use public Wi-Fi, follow these precautions:

- **Use a VPN:** A Virtual Private Network (VPN) encrypts your internet traffic, making it more secure. Install a reputable VPN app and enable it whenever you connect to public Wi-Fi.

- **Disable automatic Wi-Fi connections:** Turn off the automatic connection feature on your smartphone so that it doesn't connect to unfamiliar or potentially unsafe networks without your knowledge.

Backup Your Data

Regularly backing up your smartphone's data is crucial for two reasons: First, it ensures that your precious photos, messages, and other files are safe in case of loss or theft. Second, if your smartphone gets compromised, you can restore your data to a clean device without losing anything important.

You can back up your smartphone's data using various methods, such as:

- **Cloud storage services:** Many smartphones offer built-in options to backup your data to cloud storage services like Google Drive or iCloud.

- **External storage devices:** Connect your smartphone to a computer and copy important files to an external hard drive or USB stick.

Make data backup a regular habit to ensure you never lose important information.

Stay Vigilant

Lastly, it's essential to stay vigilant and exercise caution while using your smartphone. Here are some general tips to keep in mind:

- **Avoid suspicious links:** Be careful when clicking on links received via emails, text messages, or social media. Verify the source before opening any links.

- **Be cautious with app downloads:** Stick to reputable app stores and avoid downloading apps from unfamiliar sources, as they may contain malware or compromised software.

- **Regularly review your apps:** Periodically review the apps installed on your smartphone and uninstall any that you no longer use. This reduces the potential attack surface.

By following these recommendations, you can significantly enhance the security of your smartphone and protect your personal information from falling into the wrong hands.

Conclusion

Your smartphone is much more than just a Tinder machine; it's a digital gateway to your personal life. Securing it against cyber threats is crucial to protect your privacy and prevent unauthorized access to your personal data. By staying updated, using strong authentication, installing security apps, managing app permissions, being cautious on public Wi-Fi, backing up your data, and staying vigilant, you can fortify your smartphone in the digital Wild West. So, take control of your smartphone's security and keep your digital shit safe!

Safe Browsing: Avoiding Shady Websites Like Your Life Depends on It

In this day and age, the internet is like the Wild West. It's filled with all sorts of shady characters and questionable websites, just waiting to take advantage of unsuspecting users. But fear not, young gunslinger! In this section, we're going to arm you with the knowledge and skills to navigate the digital frontier and avoid those shady websites like your life depends on it.

Understanding the Threat Landscape

Before we dive into the nitty-gritty, let's take a moment to understand the different types of threats you may encounter while browsing the web. Just like in the real Wild West, you'll come across various dangers, each with its own unique modus operandi. Here are a few you should be aware of:

Malware: These nasty critters are designed to infiltrate your devices and wreak havoc. From viruses and worms to ransomware and Trojans, malware can do some serious damage. One wrong click on a shady website, and you could find yourself in a world of trouble.

Phishing: Think of phishing as a conman trying to trick you into giving away your personal information. These sneaky snakes will often pose as legitimate websites or services and ask you to enter your login credentials or financial details. Falling for their tricks could lead to identity theft or financial loss.

Fake Online Stores: Just like those snake oil salesmen of old, there are plenty of online stores out there trying to sell you counterfeit or non-existent products. They may have convincing websites and cheap prices, but don't be fooled!

Scams and Fraud: The internet is a breeding ground for all sorts of scams and frauds. From fake investment opportunities to "get rich quick" schemes, the digital world is filled with promises that are too good to be true.

Now that we know what we're up against, let's delve into some strategies for safe browsing.

Staying on the Right Path

1. Keep your software up to date: Outdated software, especially web browsers and plugins, can leave you vulnerable to cyber-attacks. Make sure you regularly update your software to patch any security vulnerabilities.

2. Stick to trusted websites: When it comes to browsing the internet, not all websites are created equal. Stick to well-known, reputable websites for your online activities. Websites like Amazon, Netflix, and CNN have robust security measures in place, minimizing the risk of encountering shady stuff.

3. Look for HTTPS: Whenever you're entering sensitive information, like credit card details or login credentials, always ensure that the website is encrypted using HTTPS. The "S" stands for secure and indicates that the connection between your browser and the website is encrypted, making it difficult for attackers to intercept your data.

4. Be skeptical of pop-ups and ads: Pop-up ads can be annoying, but they can also be dangerous. Some ads might redirect you to malicious websites or try to trick you into downloading malware. Avoid clicking on suspicious ads, and install ad-blockers for an extra layer of protection.

5. **Double-check URLs:** Cybercriminals are experts at creating convincing imitations of legitimate websites. Before entering any sensitive information or making a purchase, always double-check the URL to ensure it matches the official website. Look out for misspellings or slight variations that could indicate a fake website.

6. **Use a reputable antivirus software:** Antivirus software acts as a bulletproof vest for your device, protecting it from malware and other cyber threats. Invest in a reputable antivirus program and keep it updated to defend against the dangers of the digital frontier.

7. **Practice good password hygiene:** Your passwords are like the locks on your digital doors. Use unique and strong passwords for each website, and never reuse passwords across different platforms. Consider using a password manager to keep track of your login credentials securely.

8. **Be cautious with public Wi-Fi:** Public Wi-Fi networks may seem like a convenient oasis, but they can be a cyber trap. Avoid accessing sensitive information or making financial transactions while connected to public Wi-Fi. If you must use it, consider using a virtual private network (VPN) to encrypt your connection and protect your data.

A Real-Life Showdown

Let's see these strategies in action with a real-life example. Imagine you're searching for a new smartphone online, and you stumble upon a website offering the latest model at an unbelievably low price. Your cowboy senses should be tingling at this point. Here's what you should do:

1. **Investigate the website:** Check if the website you're browsing has contact information, including a physical address and customer support details. A legitimate website will provide this information for transparency and trustworthiness.

2. **Read reviews and ratings:** Look for independent reviews and ratings about the website or the product you're interested in. This can give you insights into other users' experiences and help you determine the credibility of the website.

3. **Watch out for red flags:** Take note of any suspicious signs, such as poor website design, grammatical errors, or overly aggressive sales tactics. These red flags often indicate a website that's up to no good.

4. **Verify HTTPS:** Before proceeding with any purchase, ensure that the website is secured with HTTPS. You should see a padlock symbol in the address bar, indicating a secure connection.

5. Check for secure payment options: Legitimate websites will offer reputable payment options, such as credit cards, PayPal, or trusted online payment gateways. If the website only accepts wire transfers or cryptocurrencies, it's wise to proceed with caution.

By following these steps, you can avoid falling prey to the digital outlaws on the web and make sure your online transactions are safe and secure.

Put Your Skills to the Test

Now that you've learned the ins and outs of safe browsing, it's time to put your skills to the test. Here's a little exercise to challenge your knowledge:

Scenario: You receive an email from your bank, urging you to update your account information. The email contains a link to a webpage where you're supposed to input your login credentials.

Question: What steps should you take to ensure the safety of your personal information in this situation?

Think about it for a moment, draw on the knowledge you've gained from this section, and when you're ready, check out the Solution section below.

Solution:

When faced with an email like this, it's essential to exercise caution. Here's what you should do:

1. **Don't click the link:** Avoid clicking on any links in the email, as they may redirect you to a fraudulent website.

2. **Verify the email:** Look closely at the email address of the sender. Criminals may create fake email addresses that resemble those of legitimate organizations. If in doubt, contact your bank directly using their official contact information.

3. **Visit your bank's website manually:** Open a new browser tab and type in your bank's website address directly. Once there, check for any important messages or notifications regarding your account.

4. **Report the phishing attempt:** If you're confident that the email is a phishing attempt, report it to your bank's security team. They can take appropriate action to protect other customers.

    Always remember, your bank will never ask you to provide sensitive information like passwords or Social Security numbers via email. Stay vigilant and don't fall for these tricks.

Additional Resources

Battling the dangers of the digital Wild West can be challenging, but you don't have to go it alone. Here are a few additional resources where you can learn more about safe browsing and protecting yourself online:

- Stay Safe Online - Provides tips and resources for safe internet browsing. Visit their website at https://staysafeonline.org/.

- Federal Trade Commission (FTC) - The FTC offers guidance on internet security, identity theft, and protecting your personal information. Check out their website at https://www.consumer.ftc.gov/topics/privacy-identity-online-security.

- Mozilla Firefox Blog - Regularly publishes articles on topics like safe browsing, online privacy, and tips for securing your digital life. Find them at https://blog.mozilla.org/.

Remember, the internet can be a treacherous place, but armed with the right knowledge, you can navigate the digital Wild West safely and protect your digital shit like a badass cowboy. Happy and safe browsing, partner!

Securing Your Home Network: No More Piggybacking Neighbors

In this section, we'll dive into the fascinating world of securing your home network. As more of our lives move online, it's crucial to understand the potential risks and take necessary measures to protect your digital fortress from unwanted intruders. We'll explore various strategies and best practices to ensure that your home network remains a fortress, rather than a free Wi-Fi hotspot for your nosy neighbors.

Understanding the Importance of a Secure Home Network

Before we jump into securing your home network, let's first understand why it's so important. Your home network is the gateway that connects all your devices to the internet, including your smartphones, laptops, gaming consoles, and even smart home devices. If left unprotected, it can be an easy target for cybercriminals looking to steal your personal information, infect your devices with malware, or even launch attacks on other networks.

Imagine waking up one morning to find out that your personal information, including bank account details and social media passwords, have been compromised. The consequences of a breached home network can be devastating, ranging from identity theft to financial loss. By implementing the right security measures, you can significantly reduce the chances of such nightmares becoming a reality.

Setting up a Secure Wi-Fi Network

Securing your home network starts with setting up a secure Wi-Fi network. Here are some essential steps you need to follow:

Change the Default Credentials When you purchase a new router, it usually comes with default login credentials. Don't make the rookie mistake of sticking with these defaults. Cybercriminals can easily find the default credentials online and gain unauthorized access to your network. So, change the default username and password immediately to something strong and unique that only you know.

Enable WPA2 or WPA3 Encryption Encryption is the key to ensuring that your wireless communications are secure. WPA2 (Wi-Fi Protected Access 2) and the newer standard, WPA3, provide robust encryption that makes it difficult for eavesdroppers to intercept your data. Check your router's settings and enable either WPA2 or WPA3 encryption. Avoid using WEP (Wired Equivalent Privacy), as it is outdated and can be easily cracked.

Change the Wi-Fi Network Name The Service Set Identifier (SSID), also known as the Wi-Fi network name, is often broadcasted publicly. Change the default SSID to something unique and avoid using personal information that can be easily identified, like your name or address. This step helps to make your network less attractive to potential hackers.

Use a Strong Wi-Fi Password Creating a strong Wi-Fi password is crucial in keeping unwanted guests out of your network. Follow these tips to craft a robust Wi-Fi password:

- Use a combination of uppercase and lowercase letters, numbers, and special characters.
- Make the password at least 12 characters long.
- Avoid using obvious choices like "password123" or "12345678."
- Consider using a passphrase instead of a single-word password. For example, "TheLionKing1994IsMyFav!" is much stronger and easier to remember than "P@ssw0rd123."

PROTECTING YOUR DEVICES AND NETWORKS

Implement MAC Address Filtering Every device connected to your home network has a unique Media Access Control (MAC) address. By enabling MAC address filtering on your router, you can specify which devices are allowed to connect to your network based on their MAC addresses. This adds an extra layer of security by preventing unauthorized devices from accessing your network, even if they have your Wi-Fi password.

Securing Your Router

Now that you've set up a secure Wi-Fi network, it's time to focus on securing your router itself. Here are some essential steps to take:

Regularly Update Your Router's Firmware Router manufacturers often release firmware updates to address security vulnerabilities and improve performance. Make it a habit to regularly check for firmware updates on the manufacturer's website and install them as soon as they become available. Keeping your router's firmware up to date will help protect against newly discovered exploits.

Disable Remote Management Remote management allows you to access your router's settings from anywhere on the internet. However, it also exposes a potential entry point for hackers. Unless you have a specific reason to enable remote management, it's best to disable this feature to prevent unauthorized access to your router.

Enable the Firewall A firewall acts as a barrier between your home network and the outside world, monitoring and controlling incoming and outgoing network traffic. Enable the built-in firewall on your router to add an extra layer of protection. Additionally, consider installing a software firewall on each of your devices for enhanced security.

Disable Universal Plug and Play (UPnP) Universal Plug and Play (UPnP) is a network protocol that allows devices on your network to automatically discover and communicate with each other. While convenient, UPnP can also be exploited by attackers to gain unauthorized access to your devices. Disable UPnP on your router unless you have a specific need for it.

Additional Security Measures and Best Practices

Here are some additional security measures and best practices to further safeguard your home network:

Enable Network Segmentation   Network segmentation involves dividing your home network into separate zones, each with its own security settings and access controls. By segmenting your network, you can isolate sensitive devices, like home security systems or work computers, from the rest of your network. This way, even if one device is compromised, the attacker will have a harder time moving laterally and gaining access to other devices and data.

Use a Virtual Private Network (VPN)   When accessing the internet from your home network, consider using a Virtual Private Network (VPN) to encrypt your internet traffic. A VPN creates a secure tunnel between your device and the internet, preventing eavesdroppers from intercepting your data. This is especially crucial when using public Wi-Fi networks, but it's also beneficial for protecting your privacy and security at home.

Regularly Update Your Devices   Keep all your devices, including smartphones, computers, and smart home devices, up to date with the latest security patches and firmware updates. Cybercriminals often exploit vulnerabilities in outdated software to gain unauthorized access to devices. By regularly updating your devices, you ensure that you have the latest security fixes and features.

Disable Guest Networks   Many routers offer the option to create a separate guest network, allowing visitors to access the internet without entering your main Wi-Fi password. While convenient for guests, it's best to disable this feature when not in use. Guest networks can be exploited by attackers to gain access to your home network.

Perform Regular Network Scans   Use network scanning tools to detect any unauthorized devices connected to your network. Take proactive measures to remove or block these devices to maintain the security and integrity of your home network.

Conclusion

Securing your home network is a critical step in protecting your digital shit from unwanted intruders. By following the strategies and best practices outlined in this section, you can create a robust defense against cyber threats. Remember to stay vigilant, keep your devices updated, and educate yourself about the latest security practices. With a secure home network, you can enjoy a worry-free online experience and keep those pesky piggybacking neighbors at bay.

Now that we've covered securing your home network, let's move on to the next section and explore the intriguing world of data privacy and protection.

Securing IoT Devices: From Smart Fridges to Alexa

In this section, we will delve into the wild world of IoT (Internet of Things) devices, which range from smart fridges to voice-controlled assistants like Alexa. These devices have become increasingly popular in recent years, promising convenience and a seamless integration into our daily lives. However, they also present new cybersecurity challenges that we must address to protect our digital shit.

Understanding the IoT Landscape

The IoT ecosystem consists of interconnected devices that communicate with each other and with the internet. These devices collect and exchange data, allowing us to remotely control and monitor various aspects of our homes and lives. Common IoT devices include thermostats, security cameras, smart locks, and wearable fitness trackers.

However, this convenience comes at a cost. IoT devices often lack proper security measures, making them vulnerable to cyberattacks. Manufacturers prioritize functionality and ease of use over security, resulting in weak default passwords and outdated software. As a result, hackers can exploit these vulnerabilities to gain unauthorized access to our devices and compromise our data.

Securing Your IoT Devices

Now that we understand the risks associated with IoT devices, let's explore some strategies for keeping our smart fridges, voice assistants, and other IoT gadgets secure.

1. **Keep Your Devices Up to Date:** Regularly update the firmware and software on your IoT devices. Manufacturers often release patches and security updates to address known vulnerabilities. Enable automatic updates if possible, so you don't have to worry about manually checking for updates.

2. **Change Default Credentials:** Immediately change the default usernames and passwords on your IoT devices. Hackers often have lists of default login credentials, so using them is like leaving your front door unlocked. Choose strong, unique passwords that are difficult to guess.

3. **Segment Your Network:** Create separate network segments for your IoT devices and your personal devices (laptops, smartphones, etc.). This way, even if one IoT device is compromised, the rest of your network remains secure. Many routers offer guest networks or VLAN (Virtual Local Area Network) functionality, which can help with network segmentation.

4. **Disable Unnecessary Features:** IoT devices often come with a range of features that you may not need. Disable any features or services that you don't use, as they could be potential entry points for attackers.

5. **Secure Your Home Network:** Implement strong encryption (such as WPA2 or WPA3) for your Wi-Fi network to protect your IoT devices from unauthorized access. Change the default network name (SSID) and password to prevent attackers from easily identifying and connecting to your network.

6. **Use a Secure IoT Hub:** If you have multiple IoT devices, consider using a secure IoT hub or smart home controller. These devices act as a central hub for managing your smart devices and often provide enhanced security features, such as traffic monitoring and behavior analysis.

7. **Disable Remote Access:** Unless absolutely necessary, disable remote access to your IoT devices. Limiting access to your local network reduces the potential attack surface and minimizes the risk of unauthorized access.

Real-World Examples

Let's explore a few real-world examples of IoT vulnerabilities and their consequences:

Example 1: Mirai Botnet In 2016, the Mirai botnet infected hundreds of thousands of poorly secured IoT devices, such as cameras and routers. The botnet used these devices to launch massive distributed denial-of-service (DDoS) attacks, disrupting popular websites and online services. This incident highlighted the urgent need for better IoT security.

Example 2: BlueBorne Vulnerability In 2017, security researchers discovered a critical vulnerability called BlueBorne. This vulnerability allowed attackers to take control of IoT devices using Bluetooth connections. By exploiting this vulnerability, hackers could potentially spread malware or launch targeted attacks against individuals or organizations.

Additional Resources

To further enhance your understanding of securing IoT devices, check out the following resources:

- **Website:** OWASP Internet of Things Project - The Open Web Application Security Project (OWASP) provides a comprehensive guide on securing IoT devices. Visit their website at `https://owasp.org/www-project-iot-security/`.

- **Book:** "Practical Internet of Things Security" by Brian Russell et al. - This book offers practical guidance on securing IoT devices and networks. It covers various aspects of IoT security, including risk management, device authentication, and secure communication protocols.

- **Online Course:** "Securing the Internet of Things: Best Practices for Deploying IoT Devices" - This online course, available on platforms like Coursera, provides in-depth knowledge and practical skills for securing IoT devices. Learn from industry experts and gain hands-on experience in securing various IoT components.

Exercise

Imagine you recently purchased a smart home security system with multiple IoT devices, including security cameras, motion sensors, and smart locks. Design a network architecture that ensures the security of these devices while allowing you to control and monitor them remotely. Consider the principles discussed in this section and any additional measures you find appropriate. Be ready to share your design with the class and explain your reasoning behind each architectural decision.

Conclusion

Securing IoT devices is crucial in our increasingly connected world. By following best practices, such as keeping devices up to date, changing default credentials, and segmenting networks, we can minimize the risks associated with IoT devices. Remember, protecting your digital shit means taking proactive steps to secure your smart fridges, voice assistants, and all the other connected devices in your digital wild west. Stay vigilant, Gen-Z, and may your IoT devices never fall into the hands of cyber criminals.

Social Engineering: Manipulating Human Sh*theads

Recognizing Common Social Engineering Tactics: Don't Fall for Bullsh*t

In the treacherous world of cybersecurity, social engineering tactics are like the snake oil salesmen of the digital era. These clever manipulators prey on human vulnerability and exploit our willingness to trust others. From phishing scams to impersonation attacks, they know just how to push our buttons and convince us to hand over our valuable digital shit. But fear not, my Gen-Z friends, for in this section, we'll arm you with the knowledge to spot these cunning tactics and keep your guard up against cybercriminal bullsh*t.

The Art of Manipulation: Playing on Human Psychology

Social engineering is cybercrime's answer to the Jedi mind trick. These crafty attackers use psychological manipulation to deceive individuals or organizations into acting against their own interests. By exploiting our innate human traits, such as empathy, curiosity, and the desire for recognition, these cybercriminals aim to gain unauthorized access or trick you into divulging sensitive information.

Phishing: Hook, Line, and Sinker

Picture this: You receive an email from your bank, urgently asking you to update your account details. The email looks legit, complete with the bank's logo and the threat of a frozen account if you don't comply. What do you do? Pause, take a deep breath, and ask yourself: "Is this some bullsh*t phishing attempt?"

Phishing is one of the most common social engineering tactics used today. It involves impersonating a trusted entity, such as a bank, online service provider, or even a colleague, to trick you into revealing personal information, like passwords or credit card numbers. These scams often take the form of emails, text messages, or even phone calls, luring you in with urgent requests or enticing offers.

So, how can you stay one step ahead of these phishing assholes? First off, remember this golden rule: Never click on suspicious links or download shady attachments. Instead, take a closer look at the email itself. Check the sender's email address—is it genuine or some bullsh*t imposter? Look for spelling mistakes or weird grammar—legitimate organizations usually proofread their messages. Hover your mouse over any links to see the actual URL—do they match the company's official website or are they throwing you off to Phisherville? And finally, when in doubt, contact the organization directly through their official website or customer service hotline to verify the request's authenticity.

Social Media Security: Not Everything Needs to be Shared

Ah, social media—the digital playground where we share every aspect of our lives, from adorable cat videos to our latest relationship drama. But beware, my Gen-Z comrades, for social media can also be a playground for social engineering scumbags.

When it comes to social media security, the first rule is simple: Think before you post! Avoid oversharing personal information, such as your address, full name, phone number, or birth date. These bits of information may seem innocent on their own, but in the wrong hands, they can be key pieces of the puzzle for cybercriminals to social engineer their way into your life.

Next, be cautious with accepting friend requests or connections from people you don't know. Just because someone has a cute profile picture doesn't mean they aren't some sketchy scammer trying to gather intel on you. Take the time to check their profile, mutual friends, and posts for any suspicious activity.

Another trap to watch out for on social media is the quiz or survey craze. Sure, finding out which Harry Potter character you are is fun, but these seemingly harmless quizzes may be gathering personal information about you. Be selective in the quizzes you participate in, and always check the permissions being granted to the application or website hosting the quiz.

Impersonation Attacks: When Cybercriminals Pretend to Give a Shit

Ever received a call from a charming customer service representative claiming to be from your bank, asking for your personal details? It's time to channel your inner detective, my Gen-Z warriors, because you might be dealing with an impersonation attack.

Impersonation attacks involve cybercriminals disguising themselves as trusted individuals to deceive you into giving up sensitive information. These sneaky bastards can pretend to be anyone—an employee from your bank, a colleague, a family member—in order to gain your trust and manipulate you into revealing confidential data like passwords or financial details.

So, how can you sniff out these imposters? First off, don't be quick to trust anybody who contacts you out of the blue asking for personal information. Instead, verify their identity independently. Call your bank's official customer service number or reach out to your workplace directly to confirm if the request is genuine. Remember, these attackers thrive on urgency and rely on you to act hastily, so take your time to cross-check and don't fall for their manipulative tricks.

Staying on the Defense: Social Engineering Prevention Tips

As with any wild west showdown, being prepared and vigilant is key to keeping your digital shit safe from social engineering scammers. Here are a few tips to help you stay one step ahead:

- **Educate Yourself:** Stay informed about the latest social engineering tactics and scams. Knowledge is power, my friends!

- **Think Before You Click:** Don't fall into the trap of blindly clicking on suspicious links or attachments. Take your time to assess their legitimacy.

- **Verify, Verify, Verify:** If you receive a suspicious message or request, independently verify the sender's identity using official contact channels.

- **Secure Your Privacy Settings:** Review and adjust privacy settings on social media platforms to limit the amount of personal information visible to others.

- **Stay Skeptical:** Trust your instincts and question any unexpected or unusual requests for information.

- **Report Suspicious Activity:** Help combat social engineering by reporting scams and suspicious accounts to the relevant authorities or social media platforms.

Remember, my fellow digital cowboys and cowgirls, staying savvy about social engineering is the key to protecting yourself and your digital shit from these manipulative cybercriminals. Stay alert, stay skeptical, and don't fall for their bullsh*t!

Phishing Attacks: Hook, Line, and Sinker

Phishing attacks are one of the most common and dangerous cybersecurity threats that individuals face in the digital wild west. These devious attacks rely on social engineering tactics to trick people into revealing their sensitive information, such as passwords, credit card numbers, or personal identification details. In this section, we'll dive into the world of phishing attacks, explore how they work, and learn how to protect ourselves from becoming victims of these crafty cybercriminals.

Understanding Phishing Attacks

Phishing, pronounced like "fishing," aptly describes the technique used by attackers to lure unsuspecting individuals into their traps. These attackers cast a wide net, hoping to catch as many victims as possible. They typically masquerade as trusted entities, such as banks, online retailers, or popular social media platforms, to gain the target's trust.

Phishing attacks usually come in the form of deceptive emails, text messages, or instant messages that appear to be from legitimate sources. They often leverage fear, urgency, or curiosity to prompt the recipient to take immediate action. The messages may request the victim to verify their account information, update their password, or click on a malicious link. Once the victim falls for the bait, their sensitive information is harvested and used by the cybercriminals for malicious purposes.

Recognizing Phishing Red Flags

Knowing how to identify phishing red flags is crucial in protecting yourself from falling victim to these attacks. Here are some common signs that can help you spot a phishing attempt:

- **Generic Greetings**: Phishing emails often start with generic greetings like "Dear Customer" instead of addressing you by your name. Legitimate organizations usually personalize their communications.

- **Urgency and Fear Tactics**: Phishing emails often create a sense of urgency, using phrases like "Your account will be terminated" or "Your data has been compromised." They may also threaten consequences if you fail to act immediately. Take a step back and assess the situation before clicking on any links or providing information.

- **Misspelled Words and Poor Grammar:** Phishing emails often contain spelling errors, incorrect grammar, or awkward phrasing. Legitimate organizations usually have strict quality control for their communications.

- **Suspicious Links:** Hover over any links in the email (but don't click them!) to see if the URL matches the claimed destination. Phishers often use deceptive links that lead to malicious websites. Check for subtle differences in the URL, such as misspellings or extra characters.

- **Unusual Sender Email Address:** Pay attention to the email address of the sender. Phishers may use email addresses that are similar to legitimate ones, but with slight variations. For example, they may replace the letter "o" with the number "0" or use a different domain.

Protecting Yourself Against Phishing Attacks

Now that you know how to spot a phishing attempt, let's explore some practical steps you can take to protect yourself:

- **Think Before You Click:** Be skeptical of emails or messages that require immediate action. Pause and think before clicking on any links or providing personal information. If in doubt, contact the organization directly through their official website or customer support.

- **Double Down on Security:** Make sure to keep your devices and software up to date with the latest security patches. Install reliable antivirus software and a firewall to provide an additional layer of protection against phishing attempts and other cyber threats.

- **Enable Two-Factor Authentication (2FA):** 2FA adds an extra layer of security by requiring you to provide a second form of verification, such as a unique code sent to your smartphone, in addition to your password. This makes it much harder for cybercriminals to gain access to your accounts, even if they manage to obtain your credentials.

- **Stay Informed:** Keep yourself updated about the latest phishing techniques and trends. Cybercriminals are constantly evolving, so educating yourself is an ongoing process. Follow reputable cybersecurity blogs, subscribe to security newsletters, and attend webinars or workshops to stay ahead of the game.

SOCIAL ENGINEERING: MANIPULATING HUMAN SH*THEADS

Real-World Examples

Let's take a look at a couple of real-world examples to understand the impact and consequences of falling for phishing attacks:

Example 1: The CEO Wire Transfer Scam

In this scam, attackers target employees responsible for financial transactions. They send an email that appears to be from the CEO or another high-level executive, instructing the employee to make an urgent wire transfer. The email may even mimic the CEO's writing style and use official logos to create a sense of authenticity. If the employee falls for the scam, the company could suffer significant financial losses.

Example 2: Fake Login Page

In this phishing attack, the cybercriminals create a fake login page that looks identical to a popular social media platform or an online banking portal. They send out emails or messages luring users to click on a link that directs them to this fake page. When users enter their login credentials, the attackers capture this information and gain unauthorized access to their accounts.

Take the Bait: A Phishing Attack Simulation Game

To reinforce your knowledge and test your phishing detection skills, we've included a fun and interactive game that simulates real-life phishing attacks. In this game, you'll play the role of a cybersecurity analyst and encounter various phishing emails. Your goal is to identify the fraudulent emails and avoid falling for their tricks. This game will help you sharpen your phishing detection skills and raise your awareness of common phishing tactics.

To play the game, follow this link: www.example.com/phishing-game

Remember, practice makes perfect when it comes to protecting yourself against phishing attacks. By staying vigilant and informed, you can avoid becoming just another fish in the phisher's net.

Additional Resources

- "Phishing Dark Waters: The Offensive and Defensive Sides of Malicious Emails" by Christopher Hadnagy and Michele Fincher. This book provides a deep dive into the world of phishing and offers valuable insights into the psychology behind these attacks.

- Website: www.phishing.org. This website offers information, resources, and training materials to help individuals and organizations guard against phishing attacks.

- National Cyber Security Alliance: `www.staysafeonline.org`. This organization provides resources and educational tools to promote a safer and more secure digital environment.

Remember, staying one step ahead of cybercriminals is key to protecting your digital shit. So be vigilant, question everything, and never take the phishing bait.

Social Media Security: Not Everything Needs to be Shared

In this day and age, social media has become an integral part of our lives. From sharing our personal stories and connecting with friends to promoting our businesses and expressing our opinions, social media platforms have become our virtual playgrounds. But just like any playground, there are certain rules and precautions we need to follow to ensure our safety and security. In this section, we'll dive into the world of social media security and explore why not everything needs to be shared.

The Dark Side of Social Media

Let's start by acknowledging the elephant in the room. Social media may be fun and entertaining, but it also has a dark side. Cybercriminals are constantly lurking in the shadows, ready to exploit our information for their own malicious purposes. From identity theft and phishing attacks to cyberbullying and doxing, the dangers of social media are very real.

One of the biggest challenges we face on social media platforms is the oversharing of personal information. While it may be tempting to post every detail of our lives online, we need to remember that not everything needs to be shared. Sharing too much personal information can make us vulnerable to identity theft, stalking, and other forms of online harassment.

Privacy Settings: The First Line of Defense

To protect ourselves on social media, we need to understand and effectively utilize privacy settings. Each social media platform has its own set of privacy options, and it's crucial to take the time to familiarize ourselves with them. By customizing our privacy settings, we can control who sees our posts, who can contact us, and what information is visible on our profiles.

Here are some key privacy settings to pay attention to:

- **Profile Privacy:** Adjusting the visibility of our profile to the public, friends, or a selected group of people.

- **Post Privacy:** Choosing who can see our posts, whether it's everyone, friends only, or a custom list.

- **Contact Privacy:** Managing who can send us friend requests or messages, and blocking unwanted contacts.

- **Tagging:** Controlling who can tag us in posts and photos, and whether we want to review tags before they appear on our timeline.

By regularly reviewing and updating our privacy settings, we can limit the amount of personal information exposed to the public, reducing the risk of cyber threats.

Think Before You Post: The Power of Digital Footprints

Every post, comment, like, and share on social media leaves a digital footprint. These footprints can reveal a lot about our personal lives, interests, and even our location. It's crucial to think before we post and consider the potential consequences of our actions.

Here are some important guidelines to follow:

- **Avoid Sharing Personal Information:** Don't share your address, phone number, or other sensitive information publicly. These details are like gold mines for cybercriminals.

- **Be Mindful of Geotagging:** Think twice before enabling location sharing on your posts. This information can be used to track your movements and compromise your safety.

- **Don't Expose Your Plans:** It's great to be excited about an upcoming vacation, but broadcasting your travel plans in advance can make your home a target for burglars.

- **Be Wary of Friend Requests:** When receiving friend requests from strangers, be cautious. They might have malicious intentions, such as gathering personal information or spreading malware.

Remember, once something is shared on social media, it's out there forever, even if you delete it later. Keep in mind that potential employers and educational institutions often check applicants' social media profiles, so be mindful of the image you project online.

The Role of Passwords and Two-Factor Authentication

We can't talk about social media security without addressing the importance of strong passwords and two-factor authentication (2FA).

First and foremost, **use unique and strong passwords** for all your social media accounts. Avoid using common passwords like "password123" or "123456." Instead, create complex passwords that include a combination of uppercase and lowercase letters, numbers, and symbols. Remember, the longer and more random the password, the harder it is to crack.

To enhance your account security even further, enable two-factor authentication. 2FA adds an extra layer of protection by requiring a second form of verification, typically a unique code sent to your phone or generated by an authenticator app. This way, even if someone manages to steal or guess your password, they won't be able to access your account without the second factor.

Staying Safe from Social Engineering Attacks

Social media is the perfect hunting ground for social engineering attacks. Scammers are adept at manipulating people's emotions and trust to deceive them into revealing sensitive information or clicking on malicious links. Here are a few common social engineering tactics to watch out for:

- **Phishing Messages:** Be cautious of any unsolicited messages asking for personal information or urging you to click on suspicious links. Legitimate organizations will never ask for sensitive information through direct messages.

- **Fake Reward Notifications:** If something seems too good to be true, it probably is. Beware of messages claiming that you've won a prize or a contest you didn't enter. These messages are often used to trick you into disclosing personal details.

- **Impersonation Attacks:** Cybercriminals often create fake profiles pretending to be someone you know or trust. Be skeptical of friend requests or messages from people you're already connected with. Verify their identity through an alternate means of communication before sharing any sensitive information.

Remember, your online security is just as strong as your skepticism. Think twice before trusting any message or link, and when in doubt, verify the information from a reliable source before taking any action.

Privacy and Mental Well-being

Before we wrap up this section, let's touch on the importance of balancing privacy with the well-being of our mental health. While it's essential to protect ourselves online, it's equally crucial not to isolate ourselves from the positives of social media.

Here are a few tips for finding a healthy balance:

- **Control Your News Feed:** Unfollow and mute accounts that consistently bring negativity into your life. Curate your feed to include content that uplifts and inspires you.

- **Take Breaks:** Don't let social media consume all your waking hours. Take regular breaks from scrolling and engage in real-life activities to foster personal connections and rejuvenate your mind.

- **Be Mindful of Comparison:** Remember that social media is often a highlight reel of people's lives. It's easy to fall into the comparison trap, but don't let it affect your self-esteem. Focus on your own journey and achievements.

By finding a healthy balance and being mindful of our online experiences, we can reap the benefits of social media without compromising our mental well-being.

Conclusion

In this section, we explored the importance of social media security and why not everything needs to be shared. We discussed the dark side of social media and the potential risks associated with oversharing personal information. We delved into the power of privacy settings and the importance of thinking before posting. We also touched on the significance of strong passwords, two-factor authentication, and staying vigilant against social engineering attacks. Finally, we emphasized the need to balance privacy with our mental well-being for a fulfilling online experience.

Remember, in the wild west of social media, it's crucial to protect yourself and be mindful of what you share. Stay safe, stay smart, and enjoy the benefits of the digital world without compromising your security.

Impersonation Attacks: When Cybercriminals Pretend to Give a Shit

In the vast and treacherous world of cybersecurity, there is a particular type of attack that preys on our trust and goodwill - impersonation attacks. These attacks involve cybercriminals disguising themselves as someone trustworthy or a company we know, trying to deceive us into believing that they genuinely give a shit about us. But don't be fooled! These malicious actors are only after one thing: access to your digital world so they can wreak havoc.

Understanding Impersonation Attacks

Impersonation attacks are all about deception. Cybercriminals use various techniques and methods to convincingly pose as someone or something they're not. They exploit the vulnerability of human nature and our inclination to trust others.

One common form of impersonation attack is phishing. In a phishing attack, cybercriminals send seemingly legitimate emails, text messages, or instant messages, pretending to be a trusted individual or organization. They often use social engineering tactics to manipulate our emotions, create a sense of urgency, or exploit our curiosity.

Another form of impersonation attack is spoofing. In spoofing, cybercriminals manipulate the source of an email, phone call, or website to make it appear as if it's coming from a trusted source. They might use a similar-looking domain name, display name, or phone number to deceive us into thinking it's someone we know or trust.

The Consequences of Falling for Impersonation Attacks

Falling for an impersonation attack can have severe consequences, both personally and professionally. Cybercriminals can gain unauthorized access to your accounts, steal sensitive information such as passwords, financial data, or personal identification, and use it for their malicious purposes.

For example, imagine receiving an email claiming to be from your bank, stating that there has been suspicious activity on your account and urging you to click on a link to verify your information. If you fall for this impersonation attack and provide your login credentials, the cybercriminals will have full access to your bank account and can drain your funds or perform unauthorized transactions in your name.

Impersonation attacks can also lead to identity theft. By pretending to be someone you know or trust, cybercriminals can gather enough personal information about you to impersonate you online or even in the real world. This can have long-lasting consequences, as it can damage your reputation, financial stability, and overall well-being.

Protecting Yourself from Impersonation Attacks

Now that we know how damaging impersonation attacks can be, it's crucial to arm ourselves with the knowledge and tools to protect against them. Here are some practical steps you can take to stay safe:

1. **Be skeptical:** Develop a healthy skepticism when receiving unsolicited messages or requests for personal information. Verify the authenticity of the sender before taking any action. Trust your gut, and if something feels off, it probably is.

2. **Double-check the source:** Take a close look at the email address, domain name, or phone number associated with the message. Does it match the official contact information? If there's even a slight discrepancy, be cautious.

3. **Avoid clicking on suspicious links:** Hover over links to see the actual URL before clicking on them. Make sure they lead to the correct destination. If in doubt, it's better to manually type the website address in a new browser tab rather than risk clicking on a malicious link.

4. **Don't share personal information impulsively:** Be wary of sharing personal, financial, or sensitive information without verifying the legitimacy of the request. Legitimate organizations rarely ask for such information through unsolicited messages.

5. **Enable multi-factor authentication (MFA):** MFA adds an extra layer of protection to your accounts. Even if cybercriminals manage to obtain your login credentials, they would still need an additional authentication method, such as a verification code sent to your phone, to gain access.

Remember, cybercriminals are only successful when we fall into their traps. By staying vigilant, skeptical, and informed, we can defend ourselves against impersonation attacks.

Real-World Example: CEO Fraud

An infamous example of impersonation attacks is CEO fraud. In this scenario, cybercriminals impersonate a high-ranking executive or CEO of a company and send urgent emails to employees, requesting large sums of money to be wired to a specific account. These emails are well-crafted, professionally written, and often put pressure on employees to act quickly.

Imagine you're an employee at a multinational corporation, and you receive an email from your CEO, urgently requesting a wire transfer of $100,000 for a secret acquisition. The email appears to be genuine and contains confidential company information. In a moment of panic, you comply with the request, only to find out later that it was a scam, and the money is irretrievable.

To prevent falling victim to CEO fraud or similar impersonation attacks, always verify unusual requests for money or sensitive information through a separate channel, such as a face-to-face conversation or a phone call to a known number. Maintaining a healthy level of skepticism and following established protocols is crucial in combating such attacks.

Conclusion

Impersonation attacks are crafty and calculating schemes designed to trick us into revealing sensitive information or performing actions that can harm us. By understanding the methods cybercriminals use, being skeptical, and adopting proactive security measures, we can protect ourselves from falling prey to their deceitful tactics.

Remember, the digital wild west may be full of cybercriminals masquerading as caring individuals, but with the right knowledge and mindset, you can navigate this dangerous territory and keep your shit safe. Stay alert, stay informed, and never let the impersonators fool you into thinking they give a shit.

The Wild West of Data: Privacy and Protection

Understanding Data Privacy

The Value of Personal Data: You Are Not Just a Commodity

In this section, we will explore the importance of personal data and why it is crucial to understand that we are not just commodities in the digital world. With the rise of technology and the increasing amount of personal information being collected, it is crucial to recognize the true value of our data and take steps to protect it.

Personal Data: A Modern Treasure

Personal data is the digital representation of our lives. It includes information such as our names, addresses, birthdates, social media posts, purchase history, and much more. This data is collected by various entities, including social media platforms, online retailers, government agencies, and even malicious actors.

Understanding the true value of personal data is the first step in protecting ourselves from potential harm. Our personal data has become a valuable asset that can be bought, sold, and exploited. Advertisers, data brokers, and cybercriminals all have a vested interest in obtaining our personal information for their own gain.

Why is our personal data so valuable? Well, it allows companies to target us with personalized advertisements, tailor their products and services to our preferences, and even predict our behavior. This targeted advertising generates significant revenue for companies, and in some cases, our personal data is sold to third parties without our knowledge or consent.

For cybercriminals, personal data is a goldmine. It can be used for identity theft, financial fraud, blackmail, or even extortion. By gaining access to our personal data, cybercriminals can impersonate us, access our bank accounts, or even ruin our reputations. It is important to recognize the potential harm that can arise from the misuse of personal data and take steps to protect ourselves.

The Digital Wild West: Protecting Our Personal Data

In the digital age, our personal data is constantly under threat. It is crucial to take proactive measures to protect our data and prevent it from falling into the wrong hands. Here are some key steps we can take:

1. Strengthen Your Passwords: Using strong, unique passwords for each online account is one of the simplest and most effective ways to protect your personal data. Avoid using common, easy-to-guess passwords like "123456" or "password." Instead, use a combination of uppercase and lowercase letters, numbers, and special characters.

2. Enable Two-Factor Authentication (2FA): Two-factor authentication adds an extra layer of security to your online accounts. It requires you to provide a second form of identification, such as a code sent to your phone or a fingerprint scan, in addition to your password. Enable 2FA whenever possible to protect your personal data from unauthorized access.

3. Be Mindful of Social Media: Remember that what you share on social media can be accessed by anyone. Be cautious about sharing personal information such as your address, phone number, or vacation plans. Regularly review your privacy settings and limit who can see your posts and personal information.

4. Use Encryption: Encryption is the process of converting information into a code to prevent unauthorized access. Whenever possible, use encrypted communication channels, such as websites with HTTPS and end-to-end encrypted messaging apps, to protect your personal data from interception.

5. Regularly Update and Patch Your Devices: Keeping your devices and software up to date is essential for data security. Updates often include security patches that fix vulnerabilities that cybercriminals may exploit. Set your devices to automatically install updates to ensure you have the latest security measures in place.

Data Privacy Laws: Holding Big Tech Accountable

Data privacy laws play a crucial role in protecting our personal data and holding companies accountable for how they handle it. These laws vary by country, but they typically aim to ensure that companies collect, store, and use personal data responsibly and with consent.

For example, the General Data Protection Regulation (GDPR) in the European Union has significantly strengthened data protection rights for individuals. It outlines guidelines for how companies must handle personal data, including obtaining explicit consent for data collection, providing options for data deletion, and implementing strong data security measures.

In the United States, laws such as the California Consumer Privacy Act (CCPA) and the recently enacted California Privacy Rights Act (CPRA) aim to give individuals more control over their personal data. These laws require businesses to be transparent about their data collection practices and give individuals the right to opt out of the sale of their personal information.

It is essential for individuals to be aware of their data privacy rights and hold companies accountable for how they handle personal data. By understanding these laws and advocating for stronger data protection measures, we can further safeguard our personal data and ensure that we are not just commodities in the digital world.

Conclusion

Personal data is more valuable than ever in the digital age. It can be monetized, exploited, and used against us if we are not careful. Recognizing the value of our personal data and taking steps to protect it is crucial in the digital wild west.

By strengthening our passwords, enabling two-factor authentication, being mindful of social media, using encryption, and keeping our devices up to date, we can significantly enhance our data security. Additionally, understanding data privacy laws and holding companies accountable for their handling of personal data empowers us to take control of our own digital lives.

Remember, you are not just a commodity. Your personal data has value, and it is essential to protect it in the digital wild west. Stay informed, stay vigilant, and take charge of your data security.

The Creepy World of Data Collection: The Big Brother is Watching

In the digital age, our lives are increasingly intertwined with technology. Whether we're shopping online, using social media, or even just searching for information, we leave behind a digital footprint. This footprint is made up of data that is collected by various entities, both online and offline. This data includes personal information, browsing habits, location data, and much more. Welcome to the creepy world of data collection, where Big Brother is watching your every move.

Data collection is driven by the need for companies and organizations to understand their customers and users better. They collect data to personalize our experiences, tailor advertisements to our interests, and improve their products and services. However, the extent to which data is collected and the lack of transparency about how it is used can be unsettling.

One of the biggest players in the data collection game is social media platforms. These platforms collect vast amounts of information about their users, including their demographics, interests, and online interactions. They use this data to build detailed user profiles, which are then used for targeted advertising. For example, if you've ever noticed ads for products that seem eerily relevant to your recent Google searches, congratulations, you've experienced the creepy world of data collection.

But social media platforms are not the only ones collecting data. Internet service providers (ISPs), online retailers, search engines, and mobile apps all collect data about our online activities. This data is often used to track our behavior, create personalized profiles, and sell it to third parties. In some cases, data collected by one entity can be combined with data from other sources to create an even more comprehensive picture of our lives.

So, why should you care about the creepy world of data collection? Well, apart from the obvious invasion of privacy, there are several concerning aspects to consider. First and foremost, the data collected about us can be used for nefarious purposes. It can be sold to malicious actors on the dark web, leading to identity theft, financial fraud, and even blackmail. Additionally, if this data falls into the wrong hands, it can be used to manipulate us, spread misinformation, and erode the foundations of democracy.

To protect yourself from the eyes of Big Brother, there are several steps you can take. First and foremost, be conscious of the information you share online. Be mindful of the privacy settings on your social media accounts and only share personal information with trusted entities. Use strong, unique passwords for all your online accounts and consider using a password manager to keep them secure.

Furthermore, consider using a virtual private network (VPN) to encrypt your internet traffic and hide your IP address from prying eyes. VPNs can also help you bypass location-based restrictions and protect your online activities from ISPs and other data collectors.

It's also worth considering using alternative search engines and browsers that prioritize privacy. DuckDuckGo, for example, doesn't track your searches or store any personally identifiable information. Similarly, browsers like Firefox and Brave offer built-in privacy features that block trackers and prevent websites from collecting data about you.

In conclusion, the creepy world of data collection is a reality we must face in the digital age. Our personal information is being collected, analyzed, and used to influence our lives. However, by being mindful of our online activities, understanding how data is collected and used, and taking steps to protect our privacy, we can reclaim some control over our digital identities. So, be vigilant, be informed, and remember, Big Brother may be watching, but that doesn't mean we have to let him control our lives. Stay safe out there, comrades.

Data Breaches: When Your Sh*t Hits the Fan

Data breaches are like virtual explosions that can rock your world, leaving devastation in their wake. They occur when cybercriminals infiltrate systems or networks, stealing, exposing, or manipulating sensitive data. This shit happens more often than you might think, and the consequences can be catastrophic. So buckle up, dear reader, as we dive into the wild world of data breaches and how to protect your precious digital assets.

Understanding Data Breaches

To truly comprehend the mayhem caused by data breaches, it's essential to grasp the value of personal data. In today's digital landscape, data is like currency. Companies, marketers, and hackers all want a piece of the action. Your personal data, from your name and address to your credit card details and social security number, is highly sought after.

When cybercriminals successfully breach a system, they not only gain access to this valuable information but can also manipulate or delete it. They may sell it on the dark web, use it for identity theft, or hold it for ransom. The consequences can range from financial loss and damaged reputation to emotional distress and legal troubles. It's a total shitstorm.

The Big Brother is Watching

Data collection may seem innocent at first, but it's essential to understand how your personal information is gathered, stored, and utilized. Companies often collect data to improve their products or services, tailor marketing campaigns, or even predict your behavior. However, this can morph into a creepy invasion of your privacy.

Remember when you searched for that cute pair of sneakers online, and suddenly, ads for sneakers started popping up everywhere? Yeah, that's not a coincidence. Advertisers and big tech companies are constantly monitoring your online activities, collecting data, and creating detailed profiles of your digital footprint. They know your preferences, your habits, and even your deepest secrets. It's like having a voyeuristic Big Brother constantly watching your every move.

Data Breach Fallout

When a data breach occurs, it's like a bomb exploding in the digital realm. The fallout can be massive, affecting individuals and businesses alike. Here are some of the consequences that can turn your life into a virtual nightmare:

UNDERSTANDING DATA PRIVACY

- **Identity Theft:** Your personal information can be used to open credit accounts, make purchases, or even commit crimes, all under your name. Imagine receiving calls from angry creditors demanding payment for loans you never took out or realizing that your hard-earned money has vanished from your bank account. It's enough to make you want to scream.

- **Financial Loss:** If your banking or credit card information is exposed, you may find yourself dealing with unauthorized transactions or drained accounts. Goodbye, hard-earned cash. Hello, sleepless nights and endless phone calls to your financial institutions.

- **Damaged Reputation:** When a company experiences a significant data breach, its reputation takes a nosedive. Consumers lose trust and may take their business elsewhere. Imagine finding out that a company you trusted with your personal information had failed to keep it secure. That's the kind of betrayal that hurts like a kick in the nuts.

- **Legal Troubles:** Depending on the nature of the breach, you might find yourself tangled up in legal battles. Think about potential lawsuits and the endless headaches of proving you're not guilty of the fraudulent activities committed under your name. It's like being caught in a legal shitstorm.

- **Emotional Distress:** Dealing with the aftermath of a data breach can take a toll on your mental and emotional well-being. You may feel violated, vulnerable, and anxious about the potential long-term consequences. It's the kind of stress that can keep you up at night, questioning your sanity and contemplating life's uncertainties.

Preventing Data Breaches

Now that you understand the potential havoc caused by data breaches, it's time to arm yourself with the knowledge to prevent them. While no defense is foolproof, there are steps you can take to minimize the risk of having your shit hit the fan:

- **Strengthen Your Defense:** Keep your software and operating systems up to date. Shitty developers often release patches and updates to fix security vulnerabilities. By neglecting these updates, you leave your digital fortress vulnerable to attack. So stop being a lazy ass and make sure your devices are properly fortified.

- **Beware of Phishing Attacks:** Cybercriminals are masters of deception. They'll send you carefully crafted emails or messages pretending to be from legitimate sources. These assholes try to trick you into revealing sensitive information or clicking on malicious links. Don't be a gullible dumbass; double-check the sender's identity, scrutinize the content, and never click on suspicious links. If it smells like rotten eggs, it's likely a phishing attempt.

- **Use Strong and Unique Passwords:** I can't stress this enough. Quit using "password123" or your pet's name as your password. Get creative and come up with strong, unique passwords for each account. Remember, the more complex it is, the harder it is for those damn cybercriminals to crack it. And always use a password manager to keep track of your badass passwords.

- **Enable Two-Factor Authentication (2FA):** 2FA adds an extra layer of protection to your accounts. It requires you to provide a second form of identification, usually a temporary code sent to your phone, in addition to your password. This makes it harder for attackers to infiltrate your accounts even if they get hold of your login credentials.

- **Be Wary of Public Wi-Fi:** Public Wi-Fi networks are a breeding ground for cyber scum. Avoid accessing sensitive information, such as online banking or shopping, when connected to a public network. If you must use public Wi-Fi, consider using a virtual private network (VPN) to encrypt your connection and protect your data from prying eyes.

- **Stay Informed:** Cyber threats are constantly evolving, like a never-ending dance with the devil. Stay up to date with the latest news and security practices to keep yourself one step ahead of those sneaky bastards. Subscribe to reputable cybersecurity blogs, follow experts on social media, and educate yourself on the latest trends and techniques used by cybercriminals.

Data Breach: Real-life Nightmares

Let's take a look at some infamous data breaches that left a colossal mess in their wake:

- **Equifax (2017):** One of the largest credit reporting agencies fell victim to a massive breach, exposing sensitive personal information of over 147 million Americans. It was like handing the keys to the kingdom to identity thieves, making it rain with stolen data.

- **Target (2013):** Attackers gained access to Target's network through a third-party vendor, compromising over 40 million credit and debit card accounts. Talk about a bullseye for cybercriminals.

- **Yahoo (2013-2014):** Yahoo suffered not one, but two major data breaches, affecting a staggering 3 billion user accounts. It was a giant middle finger to cybersecurity, leaving users vulnerable and screaming, "Yah-who the hell can we trust?"

- **Facebook-Cambridge Analytica (2018):** In one of the most high-profile breaches, it was revealed that Cambridge Analytica, a political consulting firm, gained access to the personal data of 87 million Facebook users without their consent. It was a digital hijacking of democracy, manipulating minds through targeted political ads.

- **Marriott (2018):** The hotel giant's reservation system was hacked, compromising the personal details of around 500 million guests. It was like checking into the Hotel California, where even after you check out, your personal information is still held captive.

Wrapping Up the Sh*tshow

Data breaches are a sad reality of our digital world. The consequences can be far-reaching, impacting individuals, businesses, and even society as a whole. As a responsible digital citizen, it's vital to stay informed, develop a cybersecurity mindset, and take steps to protect your precious data.

Remember, the Internet is akin to the Wild West, with cybercriminals lurking behind every digital corner. But armed with the knowledge and tools to defend yourself, you can be the badass gunslinger who keeps your shit safe and secure. So saddle up, dear reader, and journey into the wild frontier of cybersecurity. Your digital fortress awaits!

Data Privacy Laws: Demanding Accountability from Big Tech

In the digital age, where our personal information is increasingly being collected, stored, and exploited by big tech companies for profit, it is crucial to have robust data privacy laws that hold these companies accountable for their actions. Data privacy laws aim to protect individuals' personal data from misuse, abuse, and unauthorized access. In this section, we will explore the importance of data privacy laws and their impact on demanding accountability from big tech.

Understanding the Need for Data Privacy Laws

With the advancement of technology, personal data has become a valuable asset for companies looking to target consumers with personalized advertisements and services. However, this has also led to numerous privacy concerns, as our personal information is often shared, sold, or used without our knowledge or consent. Data privacy laws help address these concerns by setting clear rules and standards for how personal data can be collected, used, and shared. By establishing legal frameworks, these laws aim to ensure that individuals have control over their own data and can trust that it will be handled responsibly.

Key Principles of Data Privacy Laws

Data privacy laws are based on several key principles that guide their enforcement and implementation. These principles include:

1. *Consent*: Individuals must give their informed and explicit consent for the collection, processing, and sharing of their personal data. Companies are required to provide clear and transparent information about how the data will be used.

2. *Purpose Limitation*: Data should only be collected and used for specific, legitimate purposes. Companies are prohibited from using data for purposes unrelated to the original intent without obtaining additional consent.

3. *Data Minimization*: Only the minimum amount of personal data necessary for the intended purpose should be collected. Companies should avoid collecting excessive or irrelevant data.

4. *Data Security*: Companies are responsible for implementing appropriate security measures to protect the personal data they collect from unauthorized access, loss, or theft. This includes measures such as encryption, access controls, and regular security audits.

5. *Accountability*: Companies are held accountable for their data processing activities. They must be able to demonstrate compliance with data privacy laws, and individuals have the right to seek remedies if their rights are violated.

These principles form the foundation for data privacy laws and help ensure that individuals' personal data is handled in a fair, transparent, and secure manner.

Examples of Data Privacy Laws

Data privacy laws vary across countries and jurisdictions, but there are several prominent examples that have had a significant impact on demanding accountability from big tech companies. Let's take a look at two key examples:

1. **General Data Protection Regulation (GDPR):** Enacted by the European Union in 2018, GDPR is one of the most comprehensive data privacy laws to date. It applies to all companies that process the personal data of individuals within the EU, regardless of the company's location. GDPR strengthens individuals' rights by requiring explicit consent, providing the right to access and rectify personal data, and introducing strict obligations for data controllers and processors. It also imposes hefty fines for non-compliance, which has forced many big tech companies to reassess their data handling practices.

2. **California Consumer Privacy Act (CCPA):** Implemented in 2020, CCPA is the first state-level data privacy law in the United States. It gives California residents greater control over their personal data by providing the right to know what data is being collected, the right to opt-out of data sales, and the right to request deletion of personal information. CCPA applies to businesses that meet certain criteria, including having a significant presence in California or collecting data from California residents. Its introduction has prompted other states to consider similar data privacy legislation.

These examples highlight the growing recognition of the need for data privacy laws and the impact they can have on demanding accountability from big tech companies. By providing individuals with rights and ensuring consequences for non-compliance, these laws pave the way for a more privacy-conscious digital landscape.

Challenges and Future Considerations

While data privacy laws play a crucial role in demanding accountability from big tech, there are several challenges and future considerations that need to be addressed. Some of these include:

1. *Global Harmonization*: As data crosses borders, achieving global harmonization of data privacy laws becomes essential. Divergent laws across jurisdictions can create compliance challenges for multinational companies and undermine the effectiveness of individual laws.

2. *Emerging Technologies*: Advances in technology, such as artificial intelligence and Internet of Things (IoT), pose new challenges to data privacy. Future data privacy laws should be flexible and capable of adapting to these emerging technologies to provide effective protection.

3. *Enforcement and Penalties*: Ensuring effective enforcement and appropriate penalties for non-compliance is crucial for the success of data privacy laws. Stricter penalties can act as a deterrent and incentivize companies to prioritize data privacy.

As the digital landscape continues to evolve, data privacy laws must evolve with it to address emerging challenges and demands for accountability from big tech.

Conclusion

Data privacy laws play a critical role in demanding accountability from big tech by protecting individuals' personal data and establishing clear guidelines for its handling. These laws are based on key principles such as consent, purpose limitation, and data security, which aim to ensure that individuals have control over their data and can trust that it will be used responsibly. Prominent examples like GDPR and CCPA have demonstrated the impact and influence of data privacy laws on big tech companies. However, challenges remain, including the need for global harmonization and adapting to emerging technologies. By addressing these challenges and continuing to prioritize data privacy, we can create a digital environment where individuals' rights are respected, and personal data is handled with the accountability it deserves.

Safeguarding Your Online Identity

Managing Your Social Media Footprint: Don't Expose Your Sh*t

In today's digital age, social media has become an integral part of our lives. We use platforms like Facebook, Instagram, and Twitter to connect with friends, share our thoughts and experiences, and stay updated on current events. However, it's important to remember that what we post online can have real-life consequences. In this section, we will explore the concept of managing your social media footprint and why it is crucial to protect your personal information and privacy.

Understanding the Risks

When you post on social media, you are essentially leaving behind a digital trail that can be accessed by anyone, including cybercriminals, employers, and even government agencies. Your social media footprint consists of all the information you share, including personal details, photos, and your online activities. The risks associated with an unmanaged social media footprint are numerous:

- **Identity theft:** Sharing too much personal information can make it easier for cybercriminals to steal your identity and carry out fraudulent activities in your name.

- **Cyberstalking and harassment:** Revealing sensitive information or sharing your location can make you an easy target for cyberstalkers and online harassers.

- **Damaged reputation:** Inappropriate or unprofessional posts can harm your personal and professional relationships, including potential job opportunities.

- **Location-based risks:** Broadcasting your location can expose you to physical threats, such as burglaries or stalking.

- **Privacy concerns:** Social media platforms have a notorious reputation for mishandling user data. Your personal information might be shared with advertisers or other third parties without your consent.

Tips for a Responsible Digital Presence

To manage your social media footprint effectively and protect your shit, you need to be mindful of what you share and how you interact online. Here are some essential tips:

1. **Audit Your Accounts**   Regularly review and update your social media accounts' privacy settings. Each platform has different options to control who can see your posts, tag you in photos, or view your personal information. Take the time to understand these settings and customize them according to your comfort level.

2. **Think Before You Post**   Before sharing anything, ask yourself whether it can potentially harm your reputation or compromise your privacy. Be cautious about sharing personal details such as your address or contact information. Avoid posting provocative, offensive, or controversial content, as it may have negative consequences in both your personal and professional life.

3. **Limit the Personal Info You Share**   While it's essential to be genuine and authentic online, you should be selective about the personal information you share. Consider sharing only the necessary details and avoid disclosing sensitive information like your full date of birth, home address, or financial information. Remember, the fewer breadcrumbs you leave, the harder it is for someone to track you down.

4. **Be Mindful of Geotagging**   Geotagging allows social media platforms to attach your location to your posts or photos. This feature can be convenient, but it can also leave you vulnerable to real-world risks. Disable geotagging in your smartphone settings to prevent inadvertently sharing your exact location.

5. **Regularly Review Your Friends and Followers**   Take the time to review your friends or followers list, and be cautious about accepting requests from people you don't know personally. Remember, not everyone online has good intentions. Regularly prune your connections and ensure that you only share your content with people you trust.

6. **Use Strong Privacy Controls**   Utilize the privacy features offered by social media platforms to control who can view your content. For example, on platforms like Facebook, you can create custom friend lists and choose who sees specific posts. Regularly update your privacy settings as platforms often add new features or change policies.

7. **Beware of Third-Party Apps**   Be cautious about granting third-party apps access to your social media accounts. These applications may have access to your personal information or even post on your behalf. Before authorizing any app, read

their privacy policies and consider whether it's worth sharing your information with them.

8. Educate Yourself about Privacy Policies   Take the time to read and understand the privacy policies of the social media platforms you use. These policies outline how your data is collected, stored, and shared. Being aware of these policies can help you make informed decisions about what you share and with whom.

Real-World Example: The Snapchat Debacle

In 2014, Snapchat, a popular social media platform known for its disappearing messages, suffered a massive data breach. The personal information of over 4.6 million users was exposed, including names, phone numbers, and location data. The breach occurred due to a security vulnerability in the application's "Find Friends" feature. Cybercriminals exploited this flaw and gained unauthorized access to the user data.

The Snapchat incident serves as a stark reminder of the importance of managing your social media footprint. While Snapchat marketed itself as a platform for private and ephemeral messaging, the breach highlighted the potential risks associated with sharing personal data on social media.

To protect yourself from similar incidents, it's crucial to follow the tips mentioned earlier. Regularly review privacy settings, be cautious about the personal information you share, and educate yourself on the policies of the platforms you use.

Additional Resources

Managing your social media footprint is an ongoing process, and it requires staying informed about the latest privacy practices and threats. Here are some additional resources that can help you navigate the digital landscape:

- Electronic Frontier Foundation (EFF) - A nonprofit organization that defends civil liberties in the digital world. They provide resources on digital privacy and security: `https://www.eff.org/`

- PrivacyTools - A community-driven platform that offers privacy-focused tools, services, and educational content: `https://www.privacytools.io/`

- StaySafeOnline - An initiative by the National Cyber Security Alliance that provides comprehensive resources on online safety and privacy: `https://staysafeonline.org/`

Remember, managing your social media footprint is about taking control of your online presence and protecting your personal information. By being mindful about what you share and staying informed about privacy practices, you can minimize the risks and enjoy the benefits of social media without exposing your shit.

Protecting Your Online Reputation: Being a Responsible Digital Citizen

In the not-so-distant past, your reputation was mostly shaped by your actions and interactions in the real world. But in today's digital landscape, your online reputation carries significant weight. Whether you're applying for a job, seeking new friendships, or just trying to maintain a positive image, your online presence can make or break you. In this section, we'll explore the importance of protecting your online reputation and provide strategies for maintaining a responsible digital identity.

Understanding the Digital Footprint

Your digital footprint refers to the traces you leave behind while navigating the online world. Every comment you make, photo you share, or post you like contributes to your digital footprint. Just like footprints in the sand, these actions can be hard to erase.

Consider this scenario: you're in an interview for your dream job when the hiring manager decides to google your name. What will they find? Will it be a collection of well-thought-out opinions, professional accomplishments, and positive interactions, or will it be a minefield of questionable content, offensive language, and embarrassing photos? Your online reputation can have a profound impact on how others perceive you, so it's crucial to take control of your digital footprint.

Building a Positive Online Reputation

Being a responsible digital citizen means representing yourself in a way that aligns with your values and desired public image. Here are some tips for building and maintaining a positive online reputation:

- **Think before you post:** Before sharing anything online, ask yourself if it reflects the image you want to portray. Consider the potential consequences of your words and actions. If in doubt, it's best to err on the side of caution and refrain from posting.

- **Be mindful of privacy settings:** Utilize privacy settings on social media platforms to control who can see your posts and personal information. Regularly review and update these settings to ensure you're comfortable with who has access to your content.

- **Engage thoughtfully:** When interacting with others online, choose your words wisely. It's easy to get caught up in heated debates and express opinions without considering the impact they may have. Treat others with respect and engage in meaningful, constructive conversations.

- **Curate your content:** Go through your existing social media posts, photos, and comments. Remove anything that you wouldn't want potential employers, clients, or friends to see. Don't forget to regularly monitor and curate your online presence to align with your desired image.

Building a positive online reputation is an ongoing process. It requires consistent effort and self-reflection. Remember, the internet never forgets, so it's crucial to take steps to protect your digital identity.

Reacting to Negative Online Content

Despite our best efforts, negative content may still find its way into our online lives. Whether it's an offensive comment on a post or a false accusation, here are some strategies for dealing with negative online content:

- **Don't feed the trolls:** Trolls thrive on attention, so don't engage with them. Responding to negative comments often leads to prolonged arguments and further amplification of the negativity. It's best to ignore or block anyone who is intentionally trying to drag you down.

- **Report abuse:** If you come across abusive or harmful content, report it to the platform moderators or administrators. They have policies and procedures in place to address violations and may remove the content or take appropriate action against the offender.

- **Seek legal advice, if necessary:** In some cases, online harassment or defamation can have serious consequences. If you believe you've been a victim of cyberbullying or malicious intent, consult a legal professional who specializes in online defamation for guidance on next steps.

Remember that not all battles need to be fought online. Often, it's best to take a step back and prioritize your well-being over engaging in online conflicts that may do more harm than good.

Resources and Tools for Online Reputation Management

Managing your online reputation can be challenging, but luckily, there are resources and tools available to help you along the way. Here are some recommended resources:

- **Google Alerts:** Set up Google Alerts for your name, email address, or any other relevant keywords. You'll receive email notifications whenever those keywords appear online, allowing you to stay informed about your digital presence.

- **Social media management tools:** Consider using social media management tools like Hootsuite or Buffer to schedule and manage your posts across multiple platforms. These tools can help you maintain a consistent online presence while saving time.

- **Online reputation management services:** If managing your online reputation becomes overwhelming, you can enlist the help of professional services that specialize in online reputation management. These services can monitor and address any negative content, ensuring your online presence remains positive.

Additionally, staying informed about privacy settings and guidelines on various social media platforms is essential. Familiarize yourself with the options available to protect your content and limit its visibility to only those you trust.

Ethical Considerations

Being a responsible digital citizen also involves treating others' online reputations with respect. Remember that everyone has the right to privacy and deserves to have their online reputation protected. Avoid sharing or spreading harmful content, gossip, or personal information without consent.

As a society, we need to work towards creating a culture of accountability and empathy online. By being responsible digital citizens, we can contribute to a more positive and supportive digital environment for everyone.

Exercises

1. Think about the last time you posted something online without fully considering the potential consequences. What was it, and how could it have impacted your online reputation? Reflect on what you've learned from that experience and write a short paragraph discussing the lesson.

2. Imagine you come across a negative comment about yourself on a social media post. How would you respond? Write a script of your ideal response, keeping in mind the strategies mentioned in this section.

3. Research an online reputation management tool or service and write a short summary of how it works and its potential benefits for individuals looking to protect their online reputation.

Additional Resources

- Digital Citizenship: The Nine Elements of Digital Citizenship - https://www.digitalcitizenship.net/nine-elements.html

- Common Sense Education: Digital Citizenship Resources - https://www.commonsense.org/education/digital-citizenship

- ReputationDefender: Online Reputation Management Guide - https://www.reputationdefender.com/guide-online-reputation-management

Remember, protecting your online reputation is an ongoing process. By being mindful of your digital footprint, engaging in responsible online behavior, and using the resources available, you can build and maintain a positive online presence.

Doxing Attacks: When Cybercriminals Target You

In the digital wilderness of the internet, where anonymity can mask the true identity of individuals, cybercriminals often resort to doxing attacks to expose personal information and wreak havoc in the lives of unsuspecting victims. Doxing, short for "document tracing," is the malicious act of gathering and publicly revealing private information about an individual, such as their home address, phone number, social media profiles, or even sensitive documents. This section will delve into the insidious nature of doxing attacks, discuss the motivation behind such attacks, and provide you with practical tips to protect yourself from becoming a target.

Understanding the Motivations

Doxing attacks can be driven by a range of motivations, from personal vendettas to ideological conflicts. Perpetrators often carry out these attacks to intimidate, harass, or ultimately harm their victims. By exposing personal information, cybercriminals can cause significant harm, leading to real-world dangers such as stalking, identity theft, or physical harm. It is crucial to understand that no one is immune to the possibility of being doxed.

Methods and Techniques

Cybercriminals employ various methods and techniques to gather the information needed for a successful doxing attack. These can include:

- **Social Engineering:** By tricking their victims into revealing personal information, cybercriminals can exploit human vulnerabilities. They may masquerade as a trustworthy individual, such as a friend or service provider, to gain access to sensitive details.

- **OSINT (Open-Source Intelligence) Gathering:** The internet is a treasure trove of publicly available information. Cybercriminals can scour websites, social media platforms, online directories, and other sources to piece together a victim's personal information.

- **Data Breaches:** Large-scale data breaches have become increasingly common. Cybercriminals can exploit these breaches to gather a vast amount of personal data, which can then be used in doxing attacks.

- **Reverse Searching:** By using the information they already possess about a victim, cybercriminals can perform reverse searches to uncover additional details. They might use search engines, specialized online tools, or even the dark web to find hidden information.

- **Collaboration:** Cybercriminals often collaborate and share information with other malicious actors, increasing the effectiveness of their doxing attacks.

Mitigating the Risks

While the threat of doxing attacks is real, there are steps you can take to mitigate the risks and protect yourself online. Here are some practical tips:

- **Privacy Settings**: Review and adjust the privacy settings on all your online accounts, particularly social media platforms. Limit the visibility of your personal information to trusted individuals.

- **Be Mindful of What You Share**: Exercise caution when sharing personal information online, such as your address, phone number, or even your full name. Consider the potential consequences before divulging sensitive details.

- **Password Security**: Always use strong and unique passwords for all your online accounts. Enable two-factor authentication where possible to add an extra layer of security.

- **Monitor Your Online Presence**: Regularly search for your name and other identifying information online to see what others may find. This proactive approach can alert you to any potential signs of doxing.

- **Limit Public Footprint**: Be mindful of what you post and share on social media. Avoid oversharing personal details that cybercriminals could exploit. Remember, once something is on the internet, it's challenging to remove it completely.

- **Be Wary of Suspicious Requests**: Do not share personal information or engage with unknown individuals online. Be cautious of phishing attempts and avoid clicking on suspicious links or downloading untrusted files.

- **Educate Yourself**: Stay informed about the latest cybersecurity threats and techniques. By understanding common attack vectors, you can better protect yourself against doxing attacks.

- **Seek Professional Assistance**: If you believe you have become a victim of a doxing attack, reach out to law enforcement or cybersecurity professionals for assistance. They can help you navigate the complex process of dealing with the attack and minimize the potential harm.

Remember, the digital world can be a wild and unpredictable place. By adopting a proactive approach and implementing these protective measures, you can significantly reduce the risk of falling victim to doxing attacks. Stay vigilant, guard your personal information, and maintain a strong online presence that is resilient against cybercriminals who seek to exploit your private life.

Recommended Resources:

- "The Smart Girl's Guide to Privacy" by Violet Blue: A comprehensive guide that provides practical advice on protecting your privacy and security online.

- "Hiding from the Internet: Eliminating Personal Online Information" by Michael Bazzell: A step-by-step guide to removing personal information from the internet and minimizing the risk of being doxed.

- "Cybersecurity and Cyberwar: What Everyone Needs to Know" by P.W. Singer and Allan Friedman: An insightful book that explores the broad landscape of cybersecurity issues, including doxing attacks and their implications.

Exercise:

Imagine you receive an email from an unfamiliar sender claiming to have personal information about you and threatening to dox you unless you comply with their demands. Describe the steps you would take to protect yourself and minimize the potential harm. Outline the actions you would take and strategies you would employ to ensure your online safety in this situation.

Trick:

Cybersecurity is not just about protecting yourself from external threats. It also involves being mindful of your own actions and how they can inadvertently expose you to risks. Always think twice before clicking on suspicious links, sharing personal information, or engaging with strangers online. Your digital safety begins with your own behavior. Stay smart, stay safe, and be aware of the digital wilderness that surrounds you.

Encryption: Locking Sh*t Up

The Basics of Encryption: From Caesar to RSA

In this section, we will dive into the fascinating world of encryption and explore its evolution from the ancient times of Julius Caesar to the modern RSA algorithm. Encryption is a fundamental concept in cybersecurity and plays a crucial role in safeguarding our digital communications and data. So, buckle up and get ready to explore the secrets behind encryption!

A Brief History of Encryption

Encryption has been used for thousands of years as a way to secure messages and protect sensitive information. One of the earliest examples of encryption is the Caesar cipher, named after Julius Caesar, who used it to send secret military messages. The Caesar cipher is a simple substitution cipher that replaces each letter in the message with a letter a fixed number of positions down the alphabet. For example, with a shift of 3, 'A' would become 'D', 'B' would become 'E', and so on.

While the Caesar cipher was relatively easy to use, it was also easy to crack through frequency analysis. This led to the development of more complex encryption techniques over time. In the 16th century, the Vigenère cipher introduced the concept of using a keyword to determine the shifting pattern, making it harder to crack.

Fast forward to the modern era, where encryption has become highly sophisticated, thanks to advances in mathematics and computing power. One of the most widely used encryption algorithms today is RSA, named after its creators Ron Rivest, Adi Shamir, and Leonard Adleman.

The RSA Algorithm

RSA is an asymmetric encryption algorithm, meaning it uses two different keys - a public key for encryption and a private key for decryption. The security of RSA relies on the difficulty of factoring large prime numbers.

Here's a simplified version of how RSA works:

1. Key Generation: First, a user generates a pair of keys - a public key and a private key. The public key is shared with others, while the private key remains secret.

2. Encryption: If Alice wants to send a secure message to Bob, she uses Bob's public key to encrypt the message. This encrypted message can only be decrypted using Bob's private key, which only Bob possesses.

3. Decryption: Bob receives the encrypted message from Alice and uses his private key to decrypt it.

The strength of RSA lies in the difficulty of factoring large numbers. As the keys become larger, the encryption becomes exponentially stronger. This makes it extremely challenging for attackers to decrypt the message without the private key.

Real-World Applications

Encryption is used in various real-world applications to ensure the privacy and integrity of data. Let's take a look at a few examples:

1. Secure Messaging Apps: Messaging apps like Signal and WhatsApp use end-to-end encryption, which means only the sender and recipient can read the messages. Even if the messages are intercepted, they would be encrypted and useless to attackers.

2. HTTPS: When you visit a website that starts with "https://," the communication between your browser and the website is encrypted using SSL/TLS protocols. This protects your sensitive information, such as passwords and credit card details, from being intercepted.

3. Virtual Private Networks (VPNs): VPNs encrypt your internet traffic, making it difficult for third parties to monitor or intercept your online activities. This is especially important when using public Wi-Fi networks.

Key Takeaways

In this section, we explored the basics of encryption and its evolution from the Caesar cipher to the RSA algorithm. Here are the key takeaways:

- Encryption is the process of converting plaintext into ciphertext to protect information.
- The Caesar cipher and the Vigenère cipher are examples of early encryption techniques.
- RSA is a widely used asymmetric encryption algorithm that relies on large prime numbers for security.
- Real-world applications of encryption include secure messaging apps, HTTPS, and VPNs.

By understanding the basics of encryption, you are equipped with the knowledge to protect your digital communications and data in the wild west of the digital world.

Exercises

1. Research and explain how frequency analysis can be used to crack the Caesar cipher.

2. Investigate other encryption algorithms such as AES (Advanced Encryption Standard) and DES (Data Encryption Standard), and compare them to RSA.

3. Explore the concept of quantum encryption and its potential impact on cybersecurity.

4. Find a real-world example of a data breach where encryption could have prevented the exposure of sensitive information. Explain how encryption could have been implemented in that scenario.

Resources

- "The Code Book: The Science of Secrecy from Ancient Egypt to Quantum Cryptography" by Simon Singh.
  - "Introduction to Cryptography" by Johannes Buchmann.
  - "Applied Cryptography: Protocols, Algorithms, and Source Code in C" by Bruce Schneier.

Now that you have a solid understanding of the basics of encryption, it's time to delve deeper into the wild world of cybersecurity. In the next section, we will explore the fascinating realm of cloud security. Stay tuned!

End-to-End Encryption: Keeping Your Messages Private

In this digital age, where your every move is tracked, your personal data is up for grabs, and your private conversations can easily be intercepted, it's crucial to take control of your online privacy. One method that ensures the highest level of security for your messages is end-to-end encryption. In this section, we will dive deep into the concept of end-to-end encryption, how it works, and why it's so important for keeping your messages private.

Understanding Encryption Basics

Before we delve into end-to-end encryption, let's quickly refresh our minds about encryption basics. Encryption is the process of encoding information in such a way that only authorized parties can access and understand it. It involves transforming plain, readable text into an encoded format, or ciphertext, using a mathematical algorithm and a unique encryption key.

There are two main types of encryption: symmetric encryption and asymmetric encryption. In symmetric encryption, the same key is used for both encryption and decryption. It's like having a padlock that uses the same key to lock and unlock it. On the other hand, asymmetric encryption, also known as public-key encryption, uses a pair of keys: a public key for encryption and a private key for decryption. It's like having a padlock that requires a different key to lock and unlock it.

Introducing End-to-End Encryption

End-to-end encryption takes encryption to a whole new level by ensuring that only the intended recipient can decrypt and read a message. It eliminates the need for intermediaries like service providers or messaging apps to hold the encryption keys.

Instead, the keys are generated and stored locally on the sender and recipient devices, keeping the communication secure from start to finish.

Here's how it works: when you send a message using end-to-end encryption, the message is encrypted on your device using a unique encryption key. The encrypted message is then sent as ciphertext over the internet to the recipient's device. Upon receiving the ciphertext, the recipient's device uses their private key to decrypt the message, turning it back into plain, readable text.

The beauty of end-to-end encryption lies in the fact that even if a hacker manages to intercept the ciphertext during transmission, they won't be able to decipher the message without the recipient's private key. This means that your messages remain confidential and secure, even if they pass through vulnerable networks or untrustworthy service providers.

Benefits and Limitations of End-to-End Encryption

End-to-end encryption offers several important benefits for keeping your messages private:

1. Privacy: With end-to-end encryption, your messages are only readable by the intended recipient, ensuring your privacy is protected.

2. Security: By eliminating the need for intermediaries to hold encryption keys, end-to-end encryption reduces the risk of unauthorized access or data breaches.

3. Trustworthiness: End-to-end encryption allows you to communicate securely without having to rely on the trustworthiness of service providers or messaging platforms.

However, like any security measure, end-to-end encryption also has its limitations:

1. Metadata: While the content of your messages remains secure with end-to-end encryption, metadata like the sender, recipient, and timing of the communication may still be visible.

2. Device Vulnerabilities: End-to-end encryption relies on the security of the devices used for communication. If a device is compromised, the encrypted messages can still be accessed.

3. Key Management: End-to-end encryption requires careful management of encryption keys. Losing or forgetting these keys can result in permanent data loss or the inability to decrypt messages.

Real-World Applications of End-to-End Encryption

End-to-end encryption has become increasingly popular across various messaging platforms and applications. Let's take a look at some well-known examples:

1. Signal: Signal is a messaging app that offers end-to-end encryption for text messages, voice calls, and video calls. It has gained popularity among privacy-conscious individuals and activists.

2. WhatsApp: WhatsApp, one of the most widely used messaging apps globally, employs end-to-end encryption by default for all messages, voice calls, photos, and videos.

3. ProtonMail: ProtonMail is an email service that employs end-to-end encryption, ensuring that only the intended recipient can read your emails.

These examples showcase how end-to-end encryption is becoming more accessible and user-friendly, empowering individuals to take control of their digital privacy.

The Debate Over Backdoors

End-to-end encryption has not been immune to controversy. Law enforcement agencies argue that strong encryption hinders their ability to investigate criminal activities, as they are unable to access encrypted messages or data even with legal warrants.

This has led to calls for the introduction of backdoors, which would allow authorized individuals or organizations to bypass encryption and access private communications when deemed necessary. However, the inclusion of backdoors presents significant privacy and security risks, as they can potentially be exploited by malicious actors or abused by governments.

The debate over backdoors continues, highlighting the tension between privacy and national security concerns.

Conclusion

End-to-end encryption is a powerful tool for keeping your messages private in the midst of a digital landscape filled with threats and data breaches. By ensuring that only the intended recipient can decrypt and read messages, end-to-end encryption empowers individuals to take control of their digital privacy and communicate securely.

As technology continues to evolve, it's crucial to stay informed about encryption best practices and the latest advancements in secure communication. By adopting strong encryption methods and making privacy-conscious choices, you can navigate the digital wild west with confidence and protect your messages from prying eyes.

Now that we've explored the world of end-to-end encryption, let's move on to another crucial aspect of cybersecurity: cloud security. Get ready to lock down your digital playground and keep your data safe!

Encryption Tools and Apps: Fortifying Your Digital Communications

In today's digital age, where our personal and sensitive information is constantly under threat, encryption plays a vital role in safeguarding our digital communications. Encryption ensures that our messages and data are secure, protecting them from prying eyes, hackers, and cybercriminals. In this section, we will explore various encryption tools and applications that you can use to fortify your digital communications.

Understanding Encryption

To understand encryption tools and apps, let's start by diving into the basics of encryption. Encryption is the process of converting information into an unreadable form called ciphertext, making it inaccessible to unauthorized individuals. The only way to read the ciphertext is by using a secret key or passphrase to decrypt it back into its original form, known as plaintext.

There are two main types of encryption algorithms:

1. **Symmetric Encryption:** In symmetric encryption, the same key is used for both the encryption and decryption processes. This means that the sender and recipient must share the same key beforehand. Examples of symmetric encryption algorithms include Advanced Encryption Standard (AES) and Data Encryption Standard (DES).

2. **Asymmetric Encryption:** Asymmetric encryption, also known as public-key encryption, uses two different keys - a public key for encryption and a private key for decryption. The public key is widely available and can be shared with anyone, while the private key is kept secret. Examples of asymmetric encryption algorithms include RSA and Elliptic Curve Cryptography (ECC).

Encryption tools and apps leverage these encryption algorithms to provide secure communication channels and protect sensitive information.

Popular Encryption Tools and Apps

Let's explore some of the popular encryption tools and apps that can help you fortify your digital communications:

1. **Signal:** Developed by Open Whisper Systems, Signal is an encrypted messaging app that ensures end-to-end encryption for text messages, voice calls, and video calls. It uses the Signal Protocol, which provides strong security guarantees, ensuring that only the intended recipient can access your messages.

2. **Tresorit:** Tresorit is a cloud storage and collaboration platform that focuses on zero-knowledge encryption. With end-to-end encryption, Tresorit ensures that your files are encrypted locally on your device before being uploaded to their servers. This means that they have no knowledge or access to your data, providing a high level of privacy and security.

3. **ProtonMail:** ProtonMail is a secure email service that offers end-to-end encryption for your emails. Your messages are encrypted on your device before being sent to the ProtonMail servers, ensuring that even they cannot access your email contents. Additionally, ProtonMail also supports symmetric encryption for secure communication with non-ProtonMail users.

4. **Veracrypt:** Veracrypt is a powerful disk encryption software that allows you to create encrypted virtual disks and containers. You can use Veracrypt to encrypt your entire hard drive, specific folders, or even create a hidden volume within an existing volume. It provides strong encryption algorithms like AES, Serpent, and Twofish, ensuring the security of your data.

These are just a few examples of the encryption tools and apps available in the vast digital landscape. It's important to choose tools that align with your specific needs, whether it's secure messaging, cloud storage, email, or data encryption.

Best Practices for Encryption

While encryption tools and apps provide a secure foundation, it's essential to follow best practices to maximize your digital communication's fortification. Here are some tips to keep in mind:

- **Use Strong Passwords:** A strong, unique password is the first line of defense. Ensure that your passwords are lengthy, include a mix of uppercase and lowercase letters, numbers, and special characters. Avoid using easily guessable passwords like "password123" or personal information.

- **Keep Software Updated:** Encryption tools and apps regularly release updates to address security vulnerabilities and enhance performance. Make sure to keep your software up to date to benefit from the latest security patches and improvements.

- **Verify Encryption:** When using encryption tools or apps, verify that your messages or data are genuinely encrypted. Look for indicators like the padlock icon or the use of secure protocols like HTTPS to ensure secure communication channels.

- **Beware of Phishing Attacks:** Encryption can protect the content of your messages, but it can't prevent social engineering attacks. Be wary of suspicious emails, links, or requests for personal information, as these might be phishing attempts to gain unauthorized access to your data.

- **Share Encryption Keys Securely:** If you share encryption keys with others, make sure to do so in a secure and private manner. Avoid sharing encryption keys through unencrypted channels like email or public messaging platforms. Instead, consider using encrypted messaging apps or in-person key exchange.

By following these best practices, you can enhance the security of your digital communications and ensure that your sensitive information remains protected from malicious actors.

Conclusion

Encryption tools and apps are a crucial part of fortifying your digital communications. They leverage encryption algorithms to protect your messages, files, and data from unauthorized access, ensuring your privacy and security.

In this section, we explored the fundamentals of encryption, the types of encryption algorithms, and popular encryption tools and apps like Signal, Tresorit, ProtonMail, and Veracrypt. We also discussed best practices for encryption to maximize the effectiveness of these tools.

Remember, encryption is an ongoing battle between the forces of good and evil in the digital wild west. By staying informed, using secure tools, and following best practices, you can play an active role in defending your digital fortress. Stay vigilant and never underestimate the power of encryption in protecting your shit.

Cloud Security: The Digital Playground

Understanding Cloud Security Risks: Don't Get Lost in the Fog

Cloud computing has revolutionized the way we store, access, and share data. It has become an integral part of our digital lives, allowing us to store our photos, documents, and even entire applications on remote servers managed by service providers. However, with the convenience of the cloud comes a whole new set of security risks that we must be aware of and address. In this section, we will explore the potential risks associated with cloud computing and how to navigate through them without getting lost in the fog.

The Benefits of Cloud Computing

Before we dive into the risks, let's first understand why cloud computing has gained such popularity. There are several benefits that make cloud computing an attractive option:

- **Scalability:** Cloud services offer the flexibility to scale resources up or down based on demand, allowing businesses and individuals to access the computing power and storage they need at any given time.

- **Cost-effectiveness:** By moving data and applications to the cloud, organizations can reduce the need for on-premises hardware and maintenance, resulting in cost savings. Additionally, cloud providers offer pay-as-you-go pricing models, allowing users to pay only for the resources they consume.

- **Accessibility and collaboration:** Cloud computing enables easy access to data and applications from anywhere, as long as there is an internet connection. Collaboration is also simplified, as multiple users can work on the same documents simultaneously.

- **Data redundancy and disaster recovery:** Cloud service providers often have robust backup and disaster recovery mechanisms in place, ensuring that data is protected from loss due to hardware failures, natural disasters, or other unforeseen events.

While these benefits certainly make cloud computing appealing, it is important to understand that they come with their own set of risks.

Risks to Cloud Security

1. Data breaches: One of the most significant concerns with cloud computing is the potential for unauthorized access to sensitive data. Cloud service providers are responsible for securing the infrastructure, but users are responsible for securing their own data within the cloud. A data breach can occur due to weak access controls, insecure APIs, or vulnerabilities in the applications or systems used to interact with the cloud.

Example: In 2018, the Marriott hotel chain experienced a massive data breach that exposed personal information of approximately 500 million customers. The breach was attributed to a vulnerability in a web application hosted in the cloud.

2. Insider threats: Cloud service providers employ a wide range of security measures to protect customer data. However, there is always a risk of insider threats, either from malicious employees of the provider or from other users sharing the same cloud infrastructure. These threats can result in unauthorized access, data leakage, or even sabotage of other users' data.

Example: In 2016, an employee of a major cloud storage provider leaked sensitive customer data, including private photos and videos of celebrities. The incident highlighted the importance of strong access controls and monitoring for potential insider threats.

3. Compliance and legal issues: Storing data in the cloud may raise compliance and legal concerns, especially when dealing with sensitive data subject to regulations such as the Health Insurance Portability and Accountability Act (HIPAA) or the General Data Protection Regulation (GDPR). Organizations must ensure that their chosen cloud provider complies with relevant regulations and contracts, and that appropriate measures are in place to protect data privacy.

Example: A healthcare provider using a cloud service to store patient records must ensure that the cloud provider meets HIPAA requirements for maintaining the confidentiality and integrity of health information. Failure to comply could result in significant fines and damage to the provider's reputation.

Navigating the Cloud Security Maze

Now that we understand the risks associated with cloud computing, let's explore some strategies to mitigate these risks and ensure the security of our data in the cloud.

1. **Strong authentication and access controls:** Implementing strong authentication mechanisms, such as multi-factor authentication (MFA), can significantly enhance the security of cloud resources. Access controls should be carefully structured, granting the least privilege necessary for users and regularly reviewed to revoke unnecessary access.

2. **Encryption and data protection:** Encrypting data before it is uploaded to the cloud can provide an additional layer of protection, ensuring that even if the data is compromised, it remains unreadable to unauthorized parties. Cloud providers may offer encryption services, but it is crucial to understand the encryption mechanisms and key management practices employed.

3. **Regular monitoring and auditing:** Organizations should proactively monitor their cloud environments for any suspicious activities or anomalies. Logging and auditing mechanisms should be implemented to track access, changes, and potential security incidents. Cloud providers often offer monitoring tools that can be leveraged for this purpose.

4. **Vendor selection and due diligence:** When choosing a cloud service provider, it is important to conduct thorough due diligence. Consider factors such as the provider's security certifications, track record, transparency in data handling practices, and compliance with industry regulations. Additionally, ensure that a clear agreement is in place detailing the responsibilities of both parties regarding security.

5. **Employee education and awareness:** Cybersecurity awareness training should be an integral part of any organization's security program. Educate employees about the risks and best practices associated with cloud computing, emphasizing the importance of strong passwords, secure sharing, and recognizing phishing attempts.

Trick: Who said security can't be fun? Conduct regular "phishing drills" where employees are sent simulated phishing emails to test their awareness. Turn it into a friendly competition to encourage employee engagement!

Conclusion

Cloud computing presents incredible opportunities for scalability, cost savings, and accessibility. However, it also introduces new risks to the security and privacy of our data. By understanding the potential threats and implementing appropriate security measures, we can navigate through the fog of cloud security risks and confidently embrace the benefits of this innovative technology.

Resource: The Cloud Security Alliance (CSA) provides in-depth research, best practices, and tools to help organizations secure their cloud environments. Visit their website at www.cloudsecurityalliance.org for valuable resources.

Exercise: Identify three potential risks to cloud security in the context of a small e-commerce business migrating its online store to a cloud platform. Propose three mitigation strategies to address these risks.

In the next section, we will explore the basics of encryption and how it can be used to lock our digital communications and data. So tighten your seatbelts and get ready for a secure ride!

Best Practices for Securing Your Cloud Data

In today's digital world, where data breaches are as common as Kanye West's Twitter rants, securing your cloud data is of utmost importance. Whether you store your personal photos on iCloud or your business documents on Google Drive, you need to take proactive steps to protect your shit from cyber-attacks. In this section, we will explore the best practices for securing your cloud data so that you can sleep peacefully at night, knowing that your information is safe from prying eyes.

Beware of the Cloud Wild West

Before we dive into the best practices, let's take a moment to understand the risks associated with cloud computing. While the cloud offers convenience and accessibility, it also introduces new vulnerabilities that you should be aware of. Here are a few risks commonly associated with cloud computing:

- **Data breaches** - Cloud service providers may experience security breaches, leading to unauthorized access to your data.

- **Weak authentication** - Inadequate or weak authentication mechanisms can make it easier for attackers to gain access to your cloud accounts.

- **Data loss** - Technical glitches, human errors, or malicious activities can cause permanent loss of your cloud data.

- **Insider threat** - Your cloud service provider employees may have access to your data, making them potential threats if they have malicious intent.

Now that you know the potential risks, it's time to put on your sheriff hat and implement the best practices to secure your cloud data.

Strong Passwords: The First Line of Defense

Just like locking the front door of your house, having strong passwords is the first line of defense against unauthorized access. Here are some guidelines for creating strong passwords:

- **Length matters** - Aim for passwords that are at least 12 characters long. The longer, the better!

- **Mix it up** - Include a combination of uppercase and lowercase letters, numbers, and special characters in your passwords. Don't be predictable and use "Password123" as your golden key.

- **Unique is key** - Avoid reusing passwords across different cloud services. If one account gets compromised, the rest of your cloud data will still be protected.

- **Password manager** - Consider using a password manager tool to generate, store, and autofill your passwords. Just make sure to choose a reputable one with strong encryption.

Remember, a strong password is like a cowboy's lasso, making it harder for the bad guys to wrangle your data.

Two-Factor Authentication (2FA): Reinforcing the Gates

Passwords alone are not enough to keep the outlaws at bay. Two-Factor Authentication (2FA) adds an extra layer of protection by combining something you know (password) with something you have (verification code). Here's how you can implement 2FA for your cloud accounts:

- **SMS-based 2FA** - Many cloud service providers offer SMS-based 2FA, where a verification code is sent to your mobile device. While it's better than nothing, keep in mind that SMS can be intercepted or spoofed by advanced attackers.

- **Authenticator apps** - Consider using authenticator apps like Google Authenticator or Authy. These apps generate time-based verification codes that are unique to your device, making it harder for attackers to gain unauthorized access.

- **Hardware tokens** - For extra security, you can use hardware tokens, such as YubiKeys. These physical devices generate verification codes and require physical presence to authenticate.

By implementing 2FA, you're raising the drawbridge and fortifying your cloud accounts against unauthorized entry.

Encryption: Locking Shit Up

Encryption is like the Wild West's equivalent of hiding your valuables in a secret compartment. It scrambles your data into an unreadable format, ensuring that even if attackers breach your cloud service provider's defenses, they can't make sense of your precious files. Here's how you can leverage encryption to secure your cloud data:

- **Client-side encryption** - Encrypt your files locally on your device before uploading them to the cloud. This way, even if the cloud service provider experiences a breach, your data remains encrypted and unreadable without your private encryption key.

- **End-to-end encryption** - Consider using cloud storage services that offer end-to-end encryption. With end-to-end encryption, your data is encrypted on your device and can only be decrypted by the intended recipient.

- **Zero-knowledge encryption** - Look for cloud service providers that offer zero-knowledge encryption. This means that your data is encrypted in a way that the cloud service provider has no knowledge or access to your encryption keys. Only you hold the keys to unlock your shit.

By harnessing the power of encryption, you're shielding your data from prying eyes, making it as useless as a rusty old sheriff's badge in the hands of an outlaw.

Regular Backup: Safety in Numbers

Imagine a gang of bandits storming into your town and setting fire to everything. Now imagine losing all your cloud data in a catastrophic event. Scary, right? That's why you need to back up your cloud data regularly. Here are some backup best practices:

- **Automated backups** - Set up automated backups for your cloud data to ensure that you don't forget to do it manually. Schedule regular backups to a separate location or even to an offline storage device for extra protection.

- **Multiple backup locations** - Don't put all your eggs in one basket. Consider backing up your data to multiple locations, such as another cloud service

CLOUD SECURITY: THE DIGITAL PLAYGROUND

provider or an external hard drive. This way, if one backup fails, you still have another copy to rely on.

- **Test your backups** - Regularly test your backups to ensure that they are indeed functional and can be restored when needed. After all, there's no point in having backups if they don't work when shit hits the fan.

By backing up your cloud data, you're creating a safety net to catch your shit in case of a cyber-attack, just like a rodeo performer falling into a safety mattress.

Stay Updated: Be a Digital Cowboy

The cybersecurity landscape is ever-changing, with new threats and vulnerabilities popping up faster than tumbleweeds in the desert. To stay one step ahead of the bad guys, you need to keep your cloud services and devices up to date. Here's what you should do:

- **Patch management** - Enable automatic updates for your cloud services, operating systems, and applications. These updates often address security vulnerabilities and provide patches to keep your shit secure.

- **Stay informed** - Keep an eye on security news and updates from your cloud service providers. Subscribe to their security alerts or follow them on social media to stay in the know.

By staying updated, you're strapping on your spurs and riding into the sunset confidently, knowing that you've taken every precaution to secure your cloud data.

Conclusion

Securing your cloud data is not a one-time task but an ongoing commitment. By implementing strong passwords, enabling two-factor authentication, leveraging encryption, regularly backing up your shit, and staying updated, you're building strong defenses against cyber-attacks. Remember, the digital wild west is filled with outlaws and bandits looking for an opportunity to wreak havoc with your data. By following the best practices outlined in this section, you'll be well-equipped to protect your cloud data like a true digital cowboy. So saddle up, partner, and keep your cloud data safe from those pesky cyber varmints! Yeehaw!

Dealing with Cloud Data Breaches: Holding Service Providers Accountable

Cloud computing has become an integral part of our digital lives. We rely on cloud service providers to store our data, run applications, and handle our personal and business information. However, this convenience comes with its fair share of risks, including the potential for cloud data breaches. In this section, we will explore ways to hold service providers accountable for their role in protecting our data and mitigating the impact of breaches.

Understanding Cloud Data Breaches

A cloud data breach occurs when unauthorized individuals gain access to sensitive information stored in the cloud. This can happen due to various factors, such as weak security measures, insider threats, or sophisticated cyber attacks. When a breach occurs, it can have severe consequences for individuals and organizations, including financial loss, reputational damage, and violation of privacy rights.

Cloud data breaches can expose a wide range of sensitive information, including personal data, intellectual property, financial records, and trade secrets. Hackers can exploit this information for various purposes, such as identity theft, financial fraud, corporate espionage, or even extortion.

Legal Responsibilities of Cloud Service Providers

Cloud service providers have a legal and ethical responsibility to protect the data entrusted to them. While specific laws and regulations may vary across jurisdictions, there are general principles that providers must adhere to.

One important legal framework is the General Data Protection Regulation (GDPR), which governs the protection of personal data for individuals in the European Union (EU). The GDPR imposes strict requirements on cloud service providers, including the obligation to implement appropriate security measures, notify individuals and authorities in case of a breach, and maintain data protection agreements with customers.

In addition to the GDPR, several industry-specific regulations may apply to cloud service providers, such as the Health Insurance Portability and Accountability Act (HIPAA) for healthcare data or the Payment Card Industry Data Security Standard (PCI DSS) for credit card information.

Mitigating Cloud Data Breaches

While cloud service providers bear the primary responsibility for securing data, individuals and organizations must also take proactive steps to mitigate the impact of cloud data breaches.

1. **Due Diligence in Vendor Selection** Before entrusting your data to a cloud service provider, it is crucial to conduct thorough due diligence. Evaluate the provider's security practices, certifications, and reputation. Look for independent audits and security assessments to validate their claims. Taking the time to research and select a reliable and trustworthy provider can significantly reduce the risk of a data breach.

2. **Strong Access Control and Authentication Measures** Implementing robust access control and authentication measures is vital for protecting cloud data. This includes using strong passwords, multi-factor authentication (MFA), and role-based access controls. Regularly review and update access permissions to ensure that only authorized individuals have access to sensitive information.

3. **Data Encryption** Encrypting data before storing it in the cloud adds an extra layer of protection. Encryption converts data into an unreadable format, making it useless to unauthorized individuals without the encryption keys. Cloud service providers should offer encryption options, both in transit and at rest, to safeguard data from potential breaches.

4. **Incident Response Preparedness** Developing an incident response plan is crucial for minimizing the impact of a cloud data breach. This plan should outline the steps to be taken in the event of a breach, including notifying affected individuals, preserving evidence, and mitigating further damage. Regularly test and update the plan to ensure its effectiveness.

5. **Contractual Obligations and Service-Level Agreements (SLAs)** When engaging with a cloud service provider, it is essential to establish clear contractual obligations regarding data protection and breach notification. Service-Level Agreements (SLAs) should include specific provisions for breach response and remediation, including penalties for non-compliance. These contractual measures ensure that service providers are held accountable for their responsibilities.

Case Study: The Capital One Data Breach

A notable example of a cloud data breach is the Capital One data breach that occurred in 2019. The breach exposed the personal information of over 100 million Capital One customers, including social security numbers and bank account details.

The breach was the result of a misconfigured web application firewall in the cloud infrastructure. The attacker exploited this vulnerability to gain unauthorized access to sensitive data. Capital One faced significant financial and reputational repercussions, including a $80 million settlement with regulators.

The Capital One case highlights the importance of robust security measures and proactive monitoring of cloud infrastructure to prevent data breaches. It also underscores the need for cloud service providers to take responsibility for securing their systems and promptly addressing security vulnerabilities.

Resources and Further Reading

To delve deeper into the topic of cloud data breaches and holding service providers accountable, the following resources are recommended:

- Cloud Security Alliance (cloudsecurityalliance.org) - Provides guidance and best practices for securing cloud environments.

- National Institute of Standards and Technology (NIST) Special Publication 800-144 - A comprehensive guide to securing cloud computing.

- "The Big Nine: How the Tech Titans and Their Thinking Machines Could Warp Humanity" by Amy Webb - Explores the social, economic, and geopolitical impact of emerging technologies, including cloud computing and data breaches.

Key Takeaways

- Cloud data breaches can have severe consequences for individuals and organizations, including financial loss, reputational damage, and privacy violations.

- Cloud service providers have legal and ethical responsibilities to protect data. Laws such as the GDPR impose requirements on providers to implement security measures and notify individuals in case of a breach.

- Mitigating cloud data breaches involves conducting due diligence in vendor selection, implementing strong access controls and authentication measures, encrypting data, developing an incident response plan, and establishing clear contractual obligations with service providers.

- Real-world examples, such as the Capital One data breach, demonstrate the importance of proactive security measures and service provider accountability.

Now that we have explored the challenges of cloud data breaches and ways to hold service providers accountable, let's shift our focus to another critical aspect of cybersecurity: artificial intelligence. In the next section, we will delve into the potential benefits and ethical dilemmas associated with the use of AI in cyber defense.

NOTE: The content provided in this section is for educational purposes only. It should not be considered legal advice. It is recommended to consult with legal professionals and experts to ensure compliance with applicable laws and regulations.

Battling Cybercrime: Taking the Fight to the Wild West

Cybersecurity Careers: Riding Into the Sunset of Job Security

The Thrilling World of Ethical Hacking

In the exciting realm of cybersecurity, one of the most thrilling and badass roles you can find is that of an ethical hacker. These modern-day digital cowboys ride into the unknown, armed with their technical skills and a determination to protect the innocent from the malicious forces of the cyber world. In this section, we will dive deep into the thrilling world of ethical hacking and explore the strategies, tools, and mindset required to battle cybercriminals and defend our digital fortresses. So saddle up, partner, and let's ride!

What the Hell is Ethical Hacking Anyway?

Ethical hacking, also known as penetration testing or white hat hacking, is the practice of using hacking techniques to identify vulnerabilities and weaknesses in computer systems, networks, and software. Unlike our shady counterparts—the black hat hackers, who use their skills for nefarious purposes—ethical hackers are the good guys, working for individuals, organizations, or governments to find weaknesses before the bad guys do. Think of it as breaking into a building to expose its security flaws, rather than stealing shit.

Navigating the Ethical Hacking Roadmap

To become a successful ethical hacker, you need to follow a roadmap that will guide you through the skills, knowledge, and certifications required for this adrenaline-fueled profession. Buckle up, because we're about to take you on a wild ride!

1. Core Technical Skills First things first, you gotta know your shit. Ethical hackers need to have a solid understanding of computer networks, operating systems, programming languages, and common security tools. It's like being a sharpshooter, but instead of bullets, you're firing lines of code.

2. Cybersecurity Fundamentals Before you jump into the ring with cybercriminals, it's essential to grasp the concepts of cybersecurity. You need to learn about various attack vectors, encryption, the CIA Triad (no, not the government agency), and the principles of secure coding. It's like studying the tactics of outlaws so you can predict their next move.

3. Penetration Testing Methodologies Just like a gunslinger needs a plan before a shootout, an ethical hacker needs a well-defined methodology for conducting penetration tests. You'll learn about the reconnaissance phase, discovering vulnerabilities, exploiting weaknesses, and reporting your findings. It's all about outsmarting the bad guys and protecting the innocent.

4. Tools of the Trade In the wild world of ethical hacking, you'll have a vast arsenal of cutting-edge tools. From network scanners and password crackers to vulnerability assessment tools and malware analysis frameworks. These tools are like your trusty revolvers and dynamite sticks—always by your side, ready to unleash righteous havoc on the bad guys.

5. Certifications Now, it's time to prove your worth. Certifications like the Certified Ethical Hacker (CEH) and Offensive Security Certified Professional (OSCP) are your badges of honor in the world of ethical hacking. They signify that you've got the skills to pay the bills and that you're a certified badass in the eyes of employers.

The Not-So-Glamorous Side of Ethical Hacking

While it may sound like a thrilling life of high-stakes action, ethical hacking isn't all shiny gadgets and epic showdowns. There are some not-so-glamourous aspects that every aspiring ethical hacker should be aware of.

1. Legal Limitations Unlike those black hat hackers who fear no consequences, ethical hackers must operate within legal boundaries. It's like being a vigilante who fights crime but can't break the law. You'll need to familiarize yourself with the laws and regulations governing ethical hacking in your jurisdiction to avoid getting your ass locked up.

2. Staying Up to Date Cybersecurity is a domain that evolves faster than a tumbleweed on a windy day. To stay ahead of the game, ethical hackers must constantly update their knowledge and skills. It's like being a gunslinger who never puts down their revolver and always practices their aim. New attack techniques, vulnerabilities, and defense strategies emerge daily, so keeping up is key.

3. Dealing with Morally Gray Situations Sometimes, ethical hackers may find themselves in morally ambiguous situations. For example, when testing the security of a global corporation, one might uncover sensitive information that could be exploited. Balancing the need for security with personal and societal ethics can be challenging. It's like being a lone wolf who must make tough decisions to ensure the greater good.

Ethical Hacking in Action: A Real-Life Example

To better understand the thrilling world of ethical hacking, let's dive into a real-life example that showcases the skills, challenges, and impact of this exhilarating profession.

Imagine you're hired by a financial institution to perform a penetration test on their online banking system. This system allows users to access their accounts, transfer funds, and make transactions. Your mission, should you choose to accept it, is to identify any vulnerabilities that could lead to unauthorized access and theft.

You start with reconnaissance, gathering information about the bank's infrastructure, their external services, and the technologies they use. It's like stalking your prey, learning their habits, and discovering their hidden weak spots.

Next, you move on to vulnerability scanning. You use specialized software to identify any known security holes in the bank's web application, network, and database. It's like poking the enemy's armor, searching for any chinks in their defense.

Once vulnerabilities are identified, you leverage your skills to exploit them. You might try SQL injection attacks, cross-site scripting, or even social engineering techniques to gain unauthorized access. It's like sneaking into the enemy's stronghold, bypassing their guards, and reaching the treasure chamber.

Finally, you document your findings and provide recommendations to the bank on how to fix the vulnerabilities. It's like presenting a detailed report to the law enforcement agency, exposing the weaknesses of a criminal organization.

In this example, you've not only demonstrated your technical prowess but also your dedication to protecting innocent people from cybercriminals. You're a digital hero riding into the sunset, ensuring a safer and more secure digital frontier for all.

Unconventional Skill: The Art of Social Engineering

While technical skills are critical in the world of ethical hacking, there's also a lesser-known but equally powerful skill: the art of social engineering. Social engineering involves manipulating people to gain unauthorized access to sensitive information or bypass security measures. It's like being a master of persuasion, using psychology and charm to trick the unwary.

Social engineering techniques include phishing emails, impersonation, pretexting, and tailgating. By exploiting human weaknesses and trust, social engineers can convince individuals to reveal their passwords, provide access to secure areas, or share confidential information. It's like a con artist who convinces their victims to willingly hand over their valuables.

As an ethical hacker, understanding social engineering techniques is crucial. By knowing how cybercriminals manipulate people, you can educate individuals about the dangers and help them recognize and defend against these tactics. It's like being a defense attorney, always one step ahead of the prosecution.

Recommended Resources

Ready to dive deeper into the thrilling world of ethical hacking? Here are some recommended resources to level up your skills and knowledge:

Books

1. "The Web Application Hacker's Handbook" by Dafydd Stuttard and Marcus Pinto

2. "Metasploit: The Penetration Tester's Guide" by David Kennedy, Jim O'Gorman, Devon Kearns, and Mati Aharoni

3. "The Art of Deception: Controlling the Human Element of Security" by Kevin D. Mitnick and William L. Simon

Websites and Online Platforms

1. Offensive Security (https://www.offensive-security.com/)

2. Hack The Box (https://www.hackthebox.eu/)

3. OWASP (https://owasp.org/)

Remember, being an ethical hacker is not just a job—it's a calling. It's about using your powers for good, fighting the dark forces of the cyber world, and protecting innocent people from harm. So, embrace the thrill, ride into the unknown, and let the world know that you are a certified badass ethical hacker. Yeehaw!

Cybersecurity Analyst: Unmasking the Bad Guys

As the wild west of the digital world continues to grow, so does the need for cybersecurity analysts to unmask the bad guys lurking in the shadows. These modern-day sheriffs play a vital role in protecting our digital shit from cybercriminals looking to cause havoc and steal valuable information. In this section, we will dive deep into the world of cybersecurity analysis, exploring the skills, techniques, and tools used to investigate and combat cybercrime.

The Role of a Cybersecurity Analyst

Imagine yourself as a fearless detective, always on the hunt for the truth. That's what it's like to be a cybersecurity analyst. These sleuths are responsible for identifying and dissecting cyber threats, analyzing the tactics and techniques used by hackers, and devising strategies to defend against them. Think of them as the brains behind the operation, working diligently to protect individuals and organizations from imminent harm.

Investigating Cyber Attacks

Just like a crime scene investigator, a cybersecurity analyst must be well-versed in the art of forensic analysis. When an attack occurs, they are the first responders, gathering evidence, and piecing together the puzzle to identify the perpetrator. Let's take a look at the steps involved in investigating cyber attacks:

1. **Initial Assessment:** The cybersecurity analyst begins by assessing the nature and severity of the attack. They gather information about the affected systems, the type of attack, and any available logs or evidence.

2. **Data Collection:** The analyst dives deep into the digital ocean, collecting relevant data from various sources. This includes network traffic logs, system logs, timestamps, and any artifacts left behind by the attacker.

3. **Analysis:** Armed with a vast array of tools and techniques, the cybersecurity analyst analyzes the collected data to understand the attack vectors, the methods used, and the impact on the compromised systems. This step involves sifting through mountains of information, looking for patterns and anomalies that could lead to the identification of the attacker.

4. **Attribution:** Attribution is like unmasking the bad guy in a classic Western film. The cybersecurity analyst connects the dots and identifies the likely source of the attack. This involves examining the intricacies of the attack, such as the malware used, the infrastructure used for command and control, and any other indicators that may point to a specific threat actor.

5. **Reporting:** Finally, the cybersecurity analyst presents their findings in a detailed report, outlining the steps taken during the investigation and providing recommendations for preventing future attacks. This report serves as a valuable resource for organizations to strengthen their defenses and stay one step ahead of the bad guys.

Tools of the Trade

In the ever-evolving world of cybercrime, cybersecurity analysts rely on a plethora of tools to aid in their investigations. Here are some essential tools and techniques used by these digital sheriffs:

- **Network Analysis Tools:** These tools help analysts monitor network traffic, detect suspicious activities, and identify potential intrusions. Examples include Wireshark, Snort, and Zeek (formerly known as Bro).

- **Malware Analysis Tools:** Malware is a common weapon used by cybercriminals, and analysts need specialized tools to dissect and analyze malicious code. Tools like IDA Pro, Ghidra, and Cuckoo Sandbox help uncover the inner workings of malware samples.

- **Digital Forensics Tools:** Just like traditional crime scene investigators, cybersecurity analysts utilize digital forensics tools to collect and analyze evidence from compromised systems. Popular tools include EnCase, Autopsy, and Volatility Framework.

- **Threat Intelligence Platforms:** These platforms provide analysts with near-real-time information about emerging threats and known threat actors. By staying up-to-date with the latest threat intelligence, analysts can better understand the tactics and techniques used by cybercriminals.

- **Open-Source Intelligence (OSINT):** OSINT tools help analysts gather information from publicly available sources, such as social media platforms, forums, and websites. This information can provide valuable insights into the motivations and activities of threat actors.

The Cat-and-Mouse Game

Being a cybersecurity analyst is not for the faint of heart. It's a constant cat-and-mouse game, with hackers continuously evolving their tactics to outsmart defenders. To stay ahead of the bad guys, analysts must continuously update their knowledge, learn new techniques, and adapt to the changing threat landscape.

Continuous learning and professional development are essential for cybersecurity analysts. Certifications such as Certified Ethical Hacker (CEH), Certified Incident Handler (GCIH), and Certified Information Systems Security Professional (CISSP) demonstrate expertise and dedication to the field. Engaging in cybersecurity communities, attending conferences, and participating in bug bounty programs are also great ways to stay at the top of your game.

Real-World Example: The WannaCry Ransomware Attack

To illustrate the work of a cybersecurity analyst, let's look at the infamous WannaCry ransomware attack from 2017. This large-scale cyber attack affected hundreds of thousands of computers worldwide, crippling hospitals, corporations, and government institutions.

A cybersecurity analyst investigating the WannaCry attack would have followed a similar process to the one outlined earlier. They would have analyzed the malware, examined the network traffic, and deciphered the command and control infrastructure. Through meticulous investigation, they would have connected the dots to the threat actor behind the attack.

In this case, the cybersecurity community was able to attribute the attack to the Lazarus Group, a hacking group believed to be sponsored by the North Korean government. This attribution was crucial in raising awareness about the attack, improving defenses, and providing a starting point for future investigations.

Conclusion

The role of a cybersecurity analyst is vital in our increasingly connected digital world. By unmasking the bad guys, analyzing their tactics, and providing recommendations to strengthen defenses, these modern-day sheriffs are essential in protecting our digital shit. As cybercrime continues to evolve, the need for skilled and dedicated cybersecurity analysts will only grow. So saddle up, partner, and join the fight against cyber threats as a badass cybersecurity analyst.

Digital Forensics: Investigating Cybercrime like a Sherlock F*cking Holmes

In the digital wild west, where cybercriminals roam freely and wreak havoc on innocent victims, it's crucial to have modern-day Sherlock Holmeses on the case. Enter digital forensics, the badass field that specializes in investigating cybercrime and digging up the evidence needed to bring these cyber scumbags to justice.

The Art of Digital Investigation

Just like Sherlock Holmes unraveled mysteries by meticulously examining crime scenes and analyzing evidence, digital forensics involves uncovering digital footprints and analyzing data to piece together the puzzle of a cybercrime. It requires a combination of technical expertise, analytical thinking, and attention to detail.

Digital forensics investigators work closely with law enforcement agencies, private companies, and cybersecurity professionals to gather and analyze evidence related to cyber-attacks, data breaches, fraud, and other cybercrimes. Their goal is to reconstruct the sequence of events, identify the culprits, and retrieve critical information that can hold up in a court of law.

Forensic Process and Methodology

Investigating cybercrime is no walk in the park—it requires a systematic approach to ensure that no stone is left unturned. Here's a step-by-step breakdown of the digital forensic process:

1. **Identification:** The first step is to identify and define the scope of the investigation. This involves determining what needs to be investigated, the goals of the investigation, and the resources required.

2. **Preservation:** Once the scope is defined, it's time to preserve the crime scene—well, in this case, the digital crime scene. This involves creating an exact copy of the digital evidence without altering or damaging it. Specialized software and hardware tools are used to create forensic images of devices, ensuring the integrity of the evidence.

3. **Collection:** With the crime scene preserved, it's time to collect the evidence. This can include anything from hard drives, mobile devices, network traffic logs, to cloud storage. Investigators follow strict protocols to ensure the chain of custody is maintained, meaning that the evidence remains untainted and admissible in court.

4. **Analysis:** Now comes the Sherlock Holmes part—analyzing the collected evidence. Digital forensics requires expertise in a variety of areas, including data recovery, network analysis, malware analysis, and encryption. Investigators use forensic tools and techniques to examine the data, uncover hidden information, and identify patterns or anomalies that could lead to the culprits.

5. **Documentation:** In this step, investigators create detailed reports documenting their findings and methodology. This documentation is crucial for legal proceedings and can help other investigators and experts understand the methods used and the conclusions reached.

6. **Presentation:** Finally, investigators may be called upon to present their findings in court or to other stakeholders. This requires clear and concise communication, as they must effectively explain complex technical concepts to non-technical audiences.

Tools of the Trade

Digital forensics investigators have an arsenal of tools at their disposal to aid in their investigations. These tools help with tasks such as data recovery, file analysis, network monitoring, and malware detection. Some popular tools include:

- **EnCase:** A powerful digital forensic suite used for imaging, analysis, and reporting of digital evidence.
- **Autopsy:** An open-source digital forensics platform that simplifies the analysis of hard drives and smartphones.

- **Wireshark:** A network protocol analyzer that allows investigators to capture and analyze network traffic.

- **Volatility:** A memory analysis tool used to investigate the behavior of malware and extract valuable information from volatile memory.

- **Sleuth Kit:** Another open-source toolkit that provides a set of command-line tools for forensic analysis of disk images.

These tools, combined with the expertise of investigators, play a crucial role in uncovering evidence, deciphering complex attacks, and building a case against cybercriminals.

Challenges and Limitations

While digital forensics is a powerful weapon against cybercrime, it faces its fair share of challenges and limitations. Here are a few:

- **Encryption:** The increasing use of encryption makes it difficult to access and analyze data without proper decryption keys. Strong encryption algorithms can render even the most advanced forensic tools useless.

- **Anti-Forensic Techniques:** Cybercriminals are becoming more sophisticated, using anti-forensic techniques to cover their tracks and erase evidence. These techniques range from data wiping to steganography, making it harder for investigators to retrieve critical information.

- **Jurisdictional Issues:** Cybercrimes often transcend geographical boundaries, requiring international cooperation and collaboration between different law enforcement agencies. The lack of standardized procedures and cooperation can hinder investigations.

- **Rapidly Evolving Technology:** As technology advances, new devices, applications, and attack vectors emerge, posing challenges for digital forensics. Investigators must constantly adapt and stay up-to-date with the latest tools and techniques to keep pace with cybercriminals.

Despite these challenges, digital forensics remains a crucial component in the fight against cybercrime, helping to ensure that criminals are held accountable for their actions.

Real-World Example: The Sony Pictures Hack

To illustrate the role of digital forensics in investigating cybercrime, let's look at the infamous Sony Pictures hack of 2014. In this high-profile case, a group called "Guardians of Peace" targeted Sony Pictures Entertainment, leaking massive amounts of confidential data and disrupting the company's operations.

Digital forensics investigators played a vital role in uncovering the extent of the breach and identifying the perpetrators. By analyzing malware samples, network logs, and other digital evidence, they tracked the attack back to North Korea, revealing a state-sponsored cyber-attack. This investigation not only led to the identification and indictment of several individuals but also shed light on the growing threat of nation-state attacks in the cyber world.

Conclusion

Digital forensics is the modern-day Sherlock Holmes of the cyber world. Through careful investigation, analysis, and the use of specialized tools, digital forensic investigators uncover the truth and bring cybercriminals to justice. However, they face numerous challenges posed by encryption, anti-forensic techniques, jurisdictional issues, and rapidly evolving technology.

In the ongoing battle against cybercrime, digital forensics stands as a crucial line of defense, ensuring that those who violate the digital wild west are held accountable. So, if you have a burning desire to investigate cybercriminals like a badass Sherlock Fucking Holmes, digital forensics might just be the perfect career path for you.

Cybersecurity Consultant: Getting Paid to Give a Sh*t

Being a cybersecurity consultant is like being a modern-day gunslinger in the Wild West of the digital world. You ride into town, guns blazing, ready to protect the innocent from the malicious outlaws lurking in cyberspace. But instead of a trusty six-shooter, your weapon of choice is your knowledge and expertise in all things cybersecurity.

In this section, we will explore the role of a cybersecurity consultant and how you can get paid to give a shit about protecting people's digital assets. We'll discuss the skills needed, the responsibilities involved, and the challenges you might face in this exciting and ever-evolving field.

What the Hell Does a Cybersecurity Consultant Do?

A cybersecurity consultant is like a guardian angel for individuals, organizations, or even entire communities. Your job is to assess their vulnerabilities, develop strategies to mitigate risks, and implement measures to protect their digital shit from cybercriminals.

As a consultant, you will often find yourself working closely with clients to understand their unique cybersecurity needs. This could range from conducting thorough risk assessments to developing incident response plans. You'll also be responsible for training employees on cybersecurity best practices and keeping up with the latest industry trends and threats.

Skills and Expertise: More than Just Being a Computer Whiz

To be a successful cybersecurity consultant, you need more than just technical skills. While a solid foundation in computer science, networking, and programming is crucial, you must also possess a range of other qualities.

First and foremost, you need strong problem-solving skills. Cybersecurity is all about staying one step ahead of cybercriminals, so you must be able to think critically and creatively to identify vulnerabilities and develop effective countermeasures.

Communication skills are also essential. You'll be dealing with clients from different backgrounds, including those who might not have a deep understanding of technology. You need to be able to explain complex concepts in simple terms, gaining their trust and buy-in for your proposed solutions.

Furthermore, you must have a solid grasp of the legal and ethical considerations surrounding cybersecurity, as well as an understanding of relevant privacy regulations. Compliance with these regulations is critical for protecting your clients and avoiding legal trouble. Knowing when to toe the line and when to push the boundaries is part of your job.

Responsibilities and Challenges: It's Not All Fun and Games

As a cybersecurity consultant, you'll face a variety of responsibilities and challenges.

One of your main tasks will be conducting risk assessments. This involves identifying potential vulnerabilities and threats specific to your clients' systems and infrastructure. You'll then develop strategies to mitigate these risks and prioritize them based on their potential impact.

Implementing security measures is another key aspect of your role. This could involve anything from configuring firewalls and intrusion detection systems to recommending and implementing encryption protocols. You'll need to stay up-to-date with the latest cybersecurity tools and technologies to ensure your clients have the best protection available.

A major challenge you'll face is staying one step ahead of cybercriminals. Hackers are constantly evolving their strategies, finding new ways to exploit vulnerabilities. To combat this, you must maintain a proactive approach, constantly updating your knowledge and skills. Collaboration and information sharing within the cybersecurity community are essential for staying on top of emerging threats and trends.

Additionally, managing client expectations can be challenging. Many clients might expect instant and foolproof protection, but cybersecurity is an ongoing battle. You'll need to educate and communicate with your clients, helping them understand that cybersecurity is not a one-and-done deal, but an ongoing process that requires constant vigilance.

Getting Paid: Show Me the Damn Money

Now, let's talk about the sweet, sweet cash that comes with being a cybersecurity consultant. The demand for skilled professionals in this field is skyrocketing, and companies are willing to pay big bucks for your expertise.

Your earning potential as a cybersecurity consultant can vary depending on factors such as your experience, certifications, and the size and reputation of the clients you work with. On average, cybersecurity consultants can earn anywhere from $80,000 to $150,000 per year. However, top-tier consultants with extensive experience and a track record of successful projects can earn well into the six-figure range.

But it's not all about the money. As a cybersecurity consultant, you'll have the opportunity to make a real difference in the world. By protecting individuals, organizations, and even nations from cyber threats, you're contributing to a safer digital environment for everyone.

Unconventional Wisdom: The Secret Weapon of a Cybersecurity Consultant

As a cybersecurity consultant, you need all the tools and tricks up your sleeve to outsmart cybercriminals. One unconventional yet highly effective approach is leveraging the power of psychological manipulation.

Social engineering attacks, such as phishing and impersonation, often prey on human psychology and trust. By understanding how people think and behave, you can create effective countermeasures to protect against these attacks.

For example, you can conduct simulated phishing exercises within an organization to train employees to recognize and avoid phishing emails. By using psychological principles like positive reinforcement, you can turn potential victims into cybersecurity allies.

Conclusion: Become a Cybersecurity Consultant and Ride into the Sunset

Becoming a cybersecurity consultant allows you to combine your love for technology with the drive to fight against cybercriminals. With the demand for cybersecurity professionals at an all-time high, the opportunities are endless. Whether you want to work for a consulting firm, as an independent contractor, or even start your own cybersecurity business, the choice is yours.

Remember, cybersecurity is not just a job, it's a mission. By getting paid to give a shit about protecting people's digital assets, you can make a meaningful impact in the fight against cybercrime. So saddle up, partner, and ride into the digital Wild West as a cybersecurity consultant. The world needs more heroes, and you could be one of them.

Collaboration and Cooperation in the Cybersecurity Community

Information Sharing: The Power of Teamwork

In the wild world of cybersecurity, no one can go it alone. The threats we face on the digital frontier are constantly evolving, and it takes a collective effort to stay one step ahead of the bad guys. That's where information sharing comes in – the power of teamwork to combat cybercrime.

The Need for Information Sharing

Cybersecurity professionals, researchers, and organizations must share information about the latest threats, vulnerabilities, and attack methods to ensure that everyone in the community is prepared. By pooling our knowledge, we can collectively strengthen our defenses and respond more effectively to cyber threats.

Think of it as a neighborhood watch program for the digital world. Just as neighbors communicate about suspicious activities in their community to keep everyone safe, information sharing allows us to alert others to emerging threats and collaborate on finding solutions.

The Benefits of Information Sharing

1. **Early threat detection:** By sharing information about new attack vectors, malicious software, or suspicious activities, organizations can quickly identify potential threats in their own networks. This early detection allows for faster response and minimizes the damage caused by cyber attacks.

2. **Improved incident response:** When an organization falls victim to a cyber attack, sharing details of the incident, such as the attack methodology and indicators of compromise, allows others to learn from the experience and better prepare their defenses. This knowledge exchange helps the entire cybersecurity community to respond more efficiently and effectively to similar attacks in the future.

3. **Enhanced threat intelligence:** Gathering and analyzing information from multiple sources creates a more comprehensive view of the threat landscape. By combining various insights and perspectives, cybersecurity professionals can gain a deeper understanding of attackers' tactics, techniques, and procedures. This shared threat intelligence enables better decision-making and more proactive defense strategies.

4. **Strengthened partnerships:** Information sharing fosters collaboration and builds trust among organizations, professionals, and researchers in the cybersecurity community. These relationships lead to stronger partnerships, enabling joint efforts to tackle complex cyber threats. Together, we can develop innovative solutions and share best practices that benefit everyone.

Challenges and Considerations

While information sharing is crucial, it comes with its own set of challenges and considerations:

1. **Data privacy and confidentiality:** When sharing information, it's important to strike a balance between collaboration and protecting sensitive data. Organizations must ensure that personally identifiable information (PII), trade secrets, or classified information is handled with care and only shared on a need-to-know basis.

2. **Legal and regulatory barriers:** Laws and regulations surrounding data protection and privacy can create obstacles to information sharing. Organizations need to navigate these legal frameworks to determine what can be shared and how it can be done in compliance with relevant laws.

3. **Trust and transparency:** Establishing trust among participants is critical for effective information sharing. Open communication, transparency about the sources

of information, and adherence to ethical standards are essential in building trust within the cybersecurity community.

4. **Standardization and interoperability:** To effectively share information, common standards and formats are necessary. Interoperability among different cybersecurity tools, platforms, and information-sharing platforms simplifies the exchange of data and accelerates the response to threats.

Collaboration Platforms and Initiatives

To facilitate information sharing in the cybersecurity community, several platforms and initiatives have emerged:

1. **Information Sharing and Analysis Centers (ISACs):** These sector-specific organizations facilitate the exchange of cybersecurity information among organizations operating in the same industry. ISACs provide a trusted space for sharing threat intelligence, best practices, and incident response strategies.

2. **Open-source intelligence (OSINT) communities:** OSINT communities bring together cybersecurity professionals, researchers, and enthusiasts to share insights, tools, and techniques for gathering intelligence from publicly available sources. These communities leverage the power of collaboration to uncover hidden threats and vulnerabilities.

3. **Threat intelligence sharing platforms:** These platforms allow organizations to share and access threat intelligence data in a secure and standardized manner. They enable the automated exchange of indicators of compromise, threat reports, and other relevant information.

4. **Bug bounty programs:** Many organizations offer bug bounty programs, encouraging security researchers to identify and disclose vulnerabilities in their systems. These programs incentivize information sharing by rewarding researchers for their contributions.

Case Study: Operation Emotet Takedown

An excellent example of the power of information sharing is Operation Emotet Takedown, a collaborative effort to dismantle one of the world's most notorious botnets. Emotet was a modular malware that served as a delivery platform for various cyber threats, including ransomware and banking trojans.

Law enforcement agencies from multiple countries, including the United States, Canada, and European Union members, worked together with cybersecurity companies and organizations to disrupt Emotet's infrastructure.

Through coordinated actions, authorities were able to take control of the botnet's command and control servers, effectively neutralizing the threat.

The success of Operation Emotet Takedown highlights the importance of international cooperation and information sharing in combating cybercrime. By working together, we can achieve remarkable results and make the digital world a safer place.

Exercise: Build Your Information Sharing Network

To strengthen your knowledge and skills in cybersecurity, consider building your own information sharing network. Here's how:

1. Join online communities: Participate in cybersecurity forums, social media groups, and OSINT communities to connect with like-minded individuals. Engage in discussions, share insights, and learn from others' experiences.

2. Attend conferences and events: Attend cybersecurity conferences, workshops, and webinars to network with professionals in the field. These events provide opportunities to exchange ideas, learn about the latest trends, and establish connections with industry experts.

3. Collaborate on projects: Find opportunities to collaborate on cybersecurity projects with your peers. Working together on real-world challenges can enhance your skills and foster a sense of camaraderie within the community.

4. Contribute to open-source projects: Contribute to open-source cybersecurity projects by submitting code, reporting bugs, or sharing your expertise. This not only helps you improve your skills but also allows you to give back to the community.

Remember, information sharing is a two-way street. Be willing to share your own knowledge and insights while being open to learning from others. Together, we can create a stronger and more secure digital ecosystem.

The Power of Teamwork Continues

In the next section, we'll dive into the exciting world of bug bounties and how hackers are using their skills for good. Get ready to learn how the hunt for bugs can be not just a thrill but also a lucrative endeavor. Stay tuned, and keep on protecting your digital shit!

Bug Bounties: Hunting Bugs for Fun and Profit

Bug bounties have taken the cybersecurity world by storm, offering a unique opportunity for skilled hackers to hunt down vulnerabilities in exchange for fame, recognition, and cold, hard cash. In this section, we'll explore the exciting world of bug bounties, where hackers become the heroes in the fight against cybercrime.

What are Bug Bounties?

Bug bounties, also known as vulnerability reward programs, are initiatives launched by organizations to encourage hackers to find and report security vulnerabilities in their software or systems. These programs provide a legal and controlled environment for hackers to test the vulnerabilities of a system and report their findings to the organization. In return, the hackers are rewarded with hefty monetary rewards, recognition, and sometimes even swag.

Bug bounty programs have gained immense popularity in recent years, with companies such as Google, Facebook, and Microsoft offering substantial cash rewards for finding critical vulnerabilities. These programs not only help organizations discover and patch vulnerabilities before malicious actors exploit them but also allow skilled hackers to showcase their abilities and contribute to the overall security of the digital ecosystem.

The Role of Bug Hunters

Bug hunters, also known as security researchers, are the vigilantes of the cyber realm. These skilled individuals spend hours poring over code, probing systems, and testing the limits of software to uncover security weaknesses. Their main goal is to identify vulnerabilities and report them to the organization in exchange for a reward.

Bug hunters come from diverse backgrounds and possess a wide range of technical skills. Some have a deep understanding of programming languages and system architectures, while others specialize in specific areas like web application security or network infrastructure. Regardless of their expertise, bug hunters are driven by their passion for hacking and the desire to make the digital world a safer place.

The Hunt Begins: Finding Bugs

Bug hunting is both an art and a science. It requires a combination of creativity, technical expertise, and persistence. Here are some common approaches bug hunters use to find vulnerabilities:

1. **Manual Code Review:** Bug hunters meticulously review the source code of software or examine configurations to identify any coding errors or security

oversights. This process involves searching for common vulnerabilities like SQL injection, cross-site scripting, and buffer overflows.

2. **Automated Scanning:** Bug hunters leverage automated tools that scan software or systems for known vulnerabilities. These tools crawl through web applications, APIs, or networks, looking for security weaknesses. However, it's important to note that automated tools are not foolproof and often miss more subtle vulnerabilities.

3. **Fuzzing:** Fuzzing, or fuzz testing, is a technique where bug hunters input unexpected or random data into a system to identify unexpected program behaviors or crashes. By bombarding a system with unconventional inputs, bug hunters can uncover vulnerabilities that might have been missed during regular testing.

4. **Reverse Engineering:** Bug hunters use reverse engineering techniques to analyze compiled binaries, firmware, or closed-source software. By dissecting the code and understanding its inner workings, they can identify vulnerabilities that might have been intentionally hidden or overlooked.

5. **Threat Modeling:** Bug hunters think like hackers, attempting to identify potential attack vectors and weak points in a system. By understanding how an attacker might exploit a vulnerability, bug hunters can focus their efforts on specific areas and uncover hidden weaknesses.

Reporting and the Responsible Disclosure Process

Once a bug hunter has successfully identified a vulnerability, the next step is to report their findings to the organization running the bug bounty program. This process, known as responsible disclosure, ensures that the organization has time to address the vulnerability before it is made public.

Bug hunters need to follow specific guidelines provided by the organization for reporting vulnerabilities. These guidelines typically include information on what data to include in the report, how to format the report, and how to maintain confidentiality during the disclosure process.

The responsible disclosure process emphasizes the importance of collaboration between bug hunters and organizations. It allows organizations to fix vulnerabilities and improve their security posture, while bug hunters gain recognition for their findings and contribute to a safer digital environment.

Bug Bounty Platforms and Communities

Bug bounty programs are often facilitated through specialized platforms that connect bug hunters with organizations in need of security testing. These platforms offer a centralized hub for bug hunters to find and participate in bug bounty programs.

Some popular bug bounty platforms include:

- **HackerOne:** HackerOne is one of the largest bug bounty platforms, connecting bug hunters with hundreds of organizations around the world. It provides a space for bug hunters to showcase their skills, find new programs, and start hacking.

- **Bugcrowd:** Bugcrowd is another prominent bug bounty platform, hosting a wide range of bug bounty programs. It offers various challenges and competitions, making bug hunting a thrilling and competitive experience.

- **Open Bug Bounty:** Open Bug Bounty is a platform focused on public bug bounties. It allows bug hunters to report vulnerabilities to organizations that do not have formal bug bounty programs in place, encouraging a wider adoption of responsible security practices.

In addition to bug bounty platforms, bug hunters can also join online communities and forums where they can collaborate with fellow hackers, share tips and tricks, and participate in capture-the-flag (CTF) competitions. These communities provide a supportive environment to enhance skills and build connections within the cybersecurity community.

The Legal and Ethical Landscape

Bug hunting operates within a legal and ethical framework to maintain integrity and uphold the principles of responsible disclosure. Here are some key aspects to consider:

- **Terms and Conditions:** Bug hunters must carefully read and understand the terms and conditions of bug bounty programs before engaging in them. These terms outline the scope of testing, guidelines for responsible disclosure, and any legal protections provided by the organization.

- **Permission and Authorization:** Bug hunters must have explicit permission from the organization to conduct testing. Unauthorized access to systems or networks is illegal and can result in severe legal consequences.

- **Responsible Disclosure:** Bug hunters should follow the responsible disclosure process and give organizations a reasonable amount of time to address reported vulnerabilities before making them public. This ensures that organizations have an opportunity to patch vulnerabilities and safeguard their systems.

- **Coordinated Vulnerability Disclosure (CVD):** Coordinated vulnerability disclosure is a framework that promotes collaboration between bug hunters and organizations. It allows organizations to work with bug hunters to fix vulnerabilities, reducing the risk of them being exploited by malicious actors.

Bug Bounties in Action: Real-World Examples

Bug bounties have proven to be highly effective in finding and fixing vulnerabilities before they are exploited. Let's explore a couple of real-world examples to showcase their impact:

- **The United States Department of Defense (DoD):** The DoD launched its bug bounty program, "Hack the Pentagon," in 2016, with the aim of improving its security posture. The program enlisted the help of bug hunters to find vulnerabilities in its systems and rewarded them handsomely for their efforts. Bug hunters identified over 1,400 valid vulnerabilities, with the most critical issue being resolved within five hours of discovery.

- **Apple:** Apple's bug bounty program offers substantial rewards for finding vulnerabilities in its software. In 2019, a teenager discovered a vulnerability that allowed unauthorized access to users' Apple accounts. By responsibly disclosing the vulnerability through Apple's bug bounty program, the teenager not only earned a significant cash reward but also helped Apple enhance the security of its ecosystem.

These examples highlight the vital role bug hunters play in strengthening the security of organizations across various sectors.

Challenges and Rewards of Bug Hunting

While bug hunting can be thrilling and rewarding, it is not without its challenges. Bug hunters face numerous obstacles in their quest to find vulnerabilities, including complex systems, limited access, and time constraints. Additionally, competition among bug hunters can be fierce, with only the most skilled individuals standing out.

However, the rewards for successful bug hunting can be well worth the effort. Bug hunters can earn substantial financial rewards, gain recognition from the cybersecurity community, and even secure lucrative job opportunities. Bug bounties offer a unique platform for hackers to showcase their skills in an increasingly competitive industry.

Conclusion

Bug bounties have revolutionized cybersecurity by harnessing the power of ethical hacking. These programs connect skilled bug hunters with organizations in need of their expertise, resulting in enhanced security and better protection against cyber threats.

As bug hunting continues to evolve, it is more important than ever for organizations to recognize the value of bug bounties and establish robust programs. By incentivizing ethical hackers to find and report vulnerabilities, organizations can stay one step ahead of cybercriminals in this digital Wild West.

So, if you're a daring individual with a passion for hacking and an eye for detail, why not embark on a bug hunting adventure? Join a bug bounty platform, sharpen your skills, and become a cyber superhero, stopping cyber villains in their tracks, one vulnerability at a time. The Wild West of cybersecurity awaits you!

Cybersecurity Organizations and Communities: Building a Strong Network

In the Wild West of the digital world, fighting cybercrime requires a united front. Cybersecurity organizations and communities play a crucial role in building a strong network to battle against the ever-growing threats. By fostering collaboration and cooperation, these organizations bring together experts from various backgrounds to share information, exchange ideas, and develop innovative solutions. In this section, we will explore the importance of cybersecurity organizations and communities, highlighting their role in creating a united defense against cybercriminals.

The Power of Collaboration

Cybersecurity is not a one-person job. It requires the collective efforts of professionals from different domains to effectively combat cyber threats. Cybersecurity organizations provide a platform for collaboration and knowledge sharing, enabling experts to pool their resources and expertise. Through collaboration, these organizations enhance their capabilities and stay ahead of cybercriminals.

One notable example of collaboration is the Open Web Application Security Project (OWASP). OWASP is a global community-driven organization that focuses on improving the security of software. It brings together developers, security professionals, and organizations to develop tools, documentation, and standards that promote secure software development and protect against web application vulnerabilities. By sharing knowledge and best practices, OWASP empowers individuals and organizations to build secure applications and defend against evolving cyber threats.

Harnessing the Power of Bug Bounties

Bug bounties have gained significant popularity in recent years as an effective way to identify vulnerabilities in software and digital systems. Many organizations, including tech giants like Google, Microsoft, and Facebook, offer rewards to individuals or groups who discover and report security vulnerabilities. This crowdsourced approach allows organizations to leverage the collective intelligence of the cybersecurity community to strengthen their defenses.

Bug bounties not only help identify vulnerabilities but also foster a collaborative relationship between organizations and the wider cybersecurity community. By incentivizing individuals to search for vulnerabilities, organizations tap into a vast network of skilled researchers who actively contribute to their security efforts. This approach provides a win-win situation, as researchers are rewarded for finding flaws, while organizations strengthen their security posture.

Building a Strong Network of Trust

Trust is a fundamental aspect of any cybersecurity organization or community. Members must trust one another to share valuable information and insights without fear of exploitation. Building this trust requires transparency, accountability, and a commitment to the common goal of protecting digital assets and privacy.

One way to establish trust is through information sharing and threat intelligence collaboration. Organizations like the Information Sharing and Analysis Centers (ISACs) facilitate the exchange of timely and actionable cybersecurity information between industry sectors. For example, the Financial Services ISAC allows financial institutions to share critical cyber threat information to prevent and mitigate attacks effectively.

Furthermore, cybersecurity organizations and communities foster trust by promoting ethical behavior and professional standards. They encourage members to adhere to a code of conduct and ethical practices, which helps maintain integrity in the field of cybersecurity.

Resources and Opportunities for Growth

Cybersecurity organizations and communities provide a wealth of resources and opportunities for individuals looking to advance their careers in the field. They offer training programs, workshops, conferences, and certifications to enhance skills and knowledge. These resources keep cybersecurity professionals up-to-date with the latest trends, techniques, and technologies.

For instance, the SANS Institute is a leading organization that offers cybersecurity training and certifications. Their courses cover a wide range of topics, from ethical hacking to incident response, allowing professionals to specialize in their areas of interest. By participating in these programs, individuals can gain valuable insights, network with industry experts, and enhance their professional development.

Thinking Outside the Box

As cybersecurity continues to evolve, organizations and communities must embrace unconventional approaches to stay ahead of cybercriminals. In addition to traditional cybersecurity methods, such as antivirus software and firewalls, forward-thinking organizations explore innovative strategies.

One such approach is bug triage, a concept borrowed from software development. Bug triage involves prioritizing security vulnerabilities based on their severity and potential impact. By assigning the appropriate level of urgency to each vulnerability, resources can be allocated effectively, ensuring the most critical issues are addressed promptly. Bug triage not only optimizes the overall security posture but also allows organizations to focus their efforts on the most important vulnerabilities.

Conclusion

In the digital Wild West, cybersecurity organizations and communities are the backbone of a strong defense against cyber threats. By fostering collaboration, sharing knowledge, promoting ethical behavior, and providing valuable resources, these organizations build a united front against cybercriminals. By actively engaging with these communities, individuals can stay informed, expand their skills, and contribute to a safer digital environment. Together, we can create a network that ensures our digital assets remain protected in this unpredictable and ever-changing cyber landscape. So saddle up, partner! It's time to join the fight against cybercrime.

The Future of Cybersecurity

Artificial Intelligence: Friend or Foe in Cyber Defense?

Artificial Intelligence (AI) has become an integral part of our lives, from virtual assistants like Siri and Alexa to self-driving cars. In the field of cybersecurity, AI has emerged as a powerful tool to combat cyber threats. However, like any technology, it brings both benefits and risks. In this section, we will explore the role of AI in cyber defense and discuss its potential as both a friend and a foe.

The Potential of AI in Cyber Defense

AI has the potential to revolutionize cyber defense by enhancing threat detection, response, and prevention capabilities. Let's delve into some key areas where AI can make a significant impact:

1. **Threat Intelligence**: AI algorithms can analyze vast amounts of data to identify patterns, anomalies, and indicators of compromise. By continuously learning from new threats, AI systems can proactively identify emerging cyber threats and provide real-time threat intelligence to security analysts.

2. **Automated Threat Detection**: AI-powered systems can autonomously detect and classify potential threats, such as malware, phishing attempts, and intrusions. Through machine learning algorithms, AI can adapt and improve its detection capabilities over time, staying ahead of evolving cyber threats.

3. **Behavioral Analytics**: AI can monitor and analyze user behavior, network traffic, and system logs to detect suspicious activities. By establishing baseline patterns, AI can detect deviations from normal behavior, identifying potential insider threats and advanced persistent threats that traditional security measures may miss.

4. **Rapid Incident Response**: AI can aid incident response teams by automating the initial stages of incident investigation and response. By

quickly prioritizing and analyzing security events, AI can significantly reduce response times, enabling faster containment and mitigation of cyber attacks.

These advancements in the application of AI have the potential to significantly strengthen our cyber defenses, but there are also concerns regarding the risks associated with AI in cyberspace.

The Potential Risks of AI in Cyber Defense

While AI offers promising solutions, it comes with inherent risks that must be addressed. Here are some potential risks of relying on AI in cyber defense:

1. **Adversarial Attacks**: AI systems can be vulnerable to adversarial attacks, where malicious actors can exploit vulnerabilities in the AI algorithms. By manipulating input data or injecting subtle changes, adversaries can trick AI systems into misclassifying or failing to detect threats.

2. **False Positives and Negatives**: AI algorithms, although powerful, are not perfect. There is a risk of both false positives (flagging legitimate activities as threats) and false negatives (failing to detect actual threats). The effectiveness of AI systems relies heavily on the quality of data used to train them, and biases within the data can lead to inaccurate or biased conclusions.

3. **Lack of Explainability**: AI algorithms often work as black boxes, making it challenging to understand the decision-making process behind their predictions. In cybersecurity, explainability is crucial to gain trust and ensure accountability. If AI systems cannot explain why a particular action was taken or threat identified, it can lead to skepticism and hinder their adoption.

4. **Dependency and Overreliance**: Relying too heavily on AI systems can lead to a sense of complacency, assuming they can handle all threats without human intervention. This overreliance can create blind spots and vulnerabilities that attackers may exploit. Human expertise and critical thinking must remain central to cybersecurity operations.

Striking the Balance: Human-AI Collaboration

To harness the full potential of AI in cyber defense while mitigating the risks, a collaborative approach between humans and AI is essential. Here's how we can strike the right balance:

1. **Human Oversight and Expertise:** Human expertise is needed to interpret and validate the outputs of AI systems. Cybersecurity professionals play a vital role in monitoring, verifying, and fine-tuning AI algorithms to improve their accuracy and relevance. Their critical thinking skills and domain knowledge are crucial for making informed decisions based on AI-driven insights.

2. **Interpretability and Explainability:** To build trust and accountability, AI algorithms should aim to be more transparent and explainable. Research into developing interpretable AI models can help cybersecurity professionals understand how the AI arrived at certain conclusions, enabling them to make more informed decisions.

3. **Continuous Training and Learning:** AI algorithms need to be continuously updated and trained with the latest data to keep pace with ever-evolving cyber threats. Cybersecurity professionals can provide domain-specific knowledge and insights to improve the accuracy and effectiveness of AI models.

4. **Ethical Considerations:** As AI becomes more prevalent in cyber defense, ethical considerations must be at the forefront. Transparency, accountability, and privacy should remain top priorities, ensuring that AI systems are deployed responsibly and align with ethical standards.

Realizing the Potential

As the cyber landscape evolves, AI will continue to play a crucial role in cyber defense. By leveraging the strengths of AI alongside human expertise, we can better anticipate and combat cyber threats. However, it is important to navigate the risks and challenges associated with AI, ensuring that it remains a reliable and trustworthy ally in our ongoing battle against cybercrime.

In the following exercises, we will explore various real-world scenarios where AI has been used in cyber defense and discuss the potential benefits and risks in each case. Additionally, we will consider the ethical implications of integrating AI into cybersecurity operations and encourage critical thinking about the future of AI in this domain.

Now, let's dive into some exciting real-world examples that illustrate how AI is being applied in the brave new world of cyber defense.

Quantum Computing: The Game-Changer in Cryptography

In the ever-evolving landscape of cybersecurity, there is one technology that has the potential to revolutionize the field: quantum computing. With its immense processing power and ability to tackle complex calculations at lightning speed, quantum computing has the potential to break widely-used cryptographic algorithms, turning the world of cryptography on its head. In this section, we will explore the fundamental principles of quantum computing, understand its implications for cryptography, and discuss the future of secure communication in the quantum era.

Understanding Quantum Computing

To grasp the significance of quantum computing, we need to delve into the fascinating realm of quantum mechanics. Traditional computers use binary digits, or bits, which can represent either a 0 or a 1. Quantum computers, on the other hand, leverage the mind-bending principles of quantum physics to use quantum bits, or qubits. Unlike classical bits, qubits can exist in multiple states simultaneously, thanks to a property known as superposition.

Superposition allows qubits to store and process an exponentially greater amount of information compared to classical bits. This means that a quantum computer with just a few qubits has the potential to outperform even the most powerful classical supercomputers. However, harnessing the power of qubits is no easy feat, as they are highly susceptible to interference from their environment. Achieving and maintaining the delicate state of superposition is one of the greatest challenges in quantum computing.

Impact on Cryptography

The foundation of modern cryptography rests on the hardness of certain mathematical problems, such as factoring large numbers and solving discrete logarithm equations. These problems form the basis of widely-used encryption algorithms, including RSA and Diffie-Hellman. However, the extraordinary computing power of quantum computers threatens to render these algorithms obsolete.

Shor's algorithm, proposed by mathematician Peter Shor in 1994, is a quantum algorithm that can efficiently factor large numbers. Factoring large numbers is a fundamental process in many encryption schemes, including RSA. With a powerful enough quantum computer, Shor's algorithm would be able to crack RSA encryption, exposing sensitive information that is currently protected.

The implications are immense. Secure communication, online transactions, and the integrity of digital systems would all be compromised in the face of a quantum adversary. The very fabric of the digital world as we know it would unravel unless we find new and robust cryptographic algorithms that are resistant to quantum attacks.

Post-Quantum Cryptography

The race is on to develop post-quantum cryptographic algorithms that can resist the power of quantum computers. Post-quantum cryptography, also known as quantum-resistant or quantum-safe cryptography, aims to design algorithms that are secure against both classical and quantum adversaries.

One popular approach in post-quantum cryptography is lattice-based cryptography. Lattices provide a mathematical framework for constructing cryptographic functions that are believed to be quantum-resistant. These algorithms are designed to take advantage of the computational complexity inherent in solving lattice problems, making it difficult for quantum computers to gain an advantage.

Code-based cryptography is another promising avenue. It relies on error-correcting codes, which are used to encode and decode data, to create encryption schemes that are resilient to quantum attacks. The security of code-based cryptography is rooted in the hardness of decoding certain linear codes, which is believed to be computationally infeasible for quantum computers.

Other post-quantum cryptographic approaches include multivariate cryptography, hash-based cryptography, and isogeny-based cryptography. Each of these approaches has its own unique mathematical foundation and security assumptions, offering a diverse range of options for protecting our digital communications in the quantum era.

The Quantum Key Distribution Revolution

While quantum computing poses a significant threat to traditional cryptography, it also offers a potential solution: quantum key distribution (QKD). QKD utilizes the principles of quantum mechanics to establish a secure communication channel by distributing encryption keys encoded in quantum states.

The key idea behind QKD is the observer effect in quantum mechanics. Any eavesdropping or measurement on a quantum system will cause disturbance, thereby revealing the presence of an intruder. This allows the legitimate users of QKD to detect any unauthorized access attempts and ensure the confidentiality of their communication.

QKD is immune to attacks from quantum computers, as it relies on the laws of physics rather than computational complexity. It provides a provably secure method of key exchange, allowing parties to establish unbreakable encryption keys that can then be used in classical cryptographic systems.

However, QKD is not without its challenges. Practical implementations are still limited by issues such as noise, distance limitations, and compatibility with existing communication infrastructure. Nonetheless, ongoing research and technological advancements are bringing us closer to a future where secure communication through quantum key distribution becomes a reality.

Conclusion

Quantum computing is poised to disrupt the field of cryptography, rendering many of our current encryption algorithms vulnerable to attack. The race to develop quantum-resistant post-quantum cryptographic algorithms is well underway, ensuring that our digital infrastructure remains secure in the face of quantum adversaries.

Additionally, the advent of quantum key distribution provides a promising avenue for secure communication. By leveraging the principles of quantum mechanics, QKD offers a provably secure method of establishing encryption keys, protecting our sensitive information from the prying eyes of quantum computers.

As we navigate the digital wild west of the 21st century, the landscape of cybersecurity will continue to evolve. Embracing the challenges and opportunities posed by advancements in quantum computing will be crucial in safeguarding our digital world and ensuring a secure future for generations to come.

The Ethical Dilemmas of Cybersecurity Advancements

As technology continues to rapidly evolve, the field of cybersecurity faces new and complex ethical dilemmas. In this section, we will explore some of these challenging questions and dilemmas that arise from advancements in cybersecurity. It is important for Gen-Z to understand and grapple with these ethical questions as they navigate the digital landscape.

The Balancing Act: Security vs. Privacy

One of the most prominent ethical dilemmas in cybersecurity is the tension between security and privacy. With the increasing threats in the cyber world, individuals and organizations are under immense pressure to protect themselves against cyberattacks. However, many security measures involve collecting and analyzing personal data, leading to potential violations of privacy.

For example, consider the use of surveillance technologies to monitor online activities and detect potential threats. While such measures can enhance cybersecurity, they also raise concerns about the erosion of privacy and civil liberties. Striking the right balance between security and privacy is a difficult task, as it requires careful consideration of the potential benefits and harms.

The Dark Side of Artificial Intelligence

Artificial Intelligence (AI) holds great promise for enhancing cybersecurity. Machine learning algorithms can analyze vast amounts of data and detect patterns that humans may overlook. However, the use of AI in cybersecurity also presents ethical challenges.

One of the ethical dilemmas arises from the potential for biased decision-making. AI algorithms learn from existing data, which may be biased or reflect societal prejudices. If these biases are embedded in the algorithms used for cybersecurity, it may result in discriminatory practices or false accusations.

Moreover, the use of AI in offensive cyber operations raises ethical concerns. AI-powered cyber weapons can autonomously target and attack vulnerabilities in computer systems. This raises questions about accountability and the potential for unintended consequences, as AI may not always make ethical judgments in complex scenarios.

Hacking Back: Vigilantism or Self-Defense?

When organizations fall victim to cyberattacks, they face a difficult decision: should they retaliate or take defensive measures only? The concept of "hacking back" refers to the practice of actively targeting and disabling cyber attackers.

While hacking back may seem like a form of vigilantism, some argue that it is a legitimate form of self-defense. However, this raises ethical questions about the potential for collateral damage and escalating cyber conflicts. Without international norms and regulations governing hacking back, it can quickly devolve into a digital Wild West.

Cybersecurity for Whom?

Another ethical dilemma in cybersecurity lies in the unequal distribution of cybersecurity resources. While large organizations can afford advanced security measures and employ cybersecurity experts, individuals and small businesses often lack the necessary resources and expertise to protect themselves adequately.

This imbalance raises questions of fairness and social justice. How can we ensure that cybersecurity advancements are accessible to all, regardless of their socioeconomic status? Bridging this gap requires a collective effort from policymakers, industry leaders, and the cybersecurity community to provide affordable and user-friendly security solutions.

The Human Element: Ethical Hacking and Responsible Disclosure

Ethical hacking, also known as "white hat hacking," refers to the practice of intentionally probing computer systems to identify vulnerabilities and patch them before malicious hackers can exploit them. While ethical hacking plays a crucial role in enhancing cybersecurity, it comes with its own set of ethical dilemmas.

For example, ethical hackers often discover vulnerabilities in widely used software or digital services. The ethical dilemma arises when deciding whether, when, and how to disclose these vulnerabilities to the developers or the public. Premature disclosure can potentially allow malicious actors to exploit the vulnerabilities, while delaying disclosure may leave users exposed for longer periods.

Responsible disclosure practices aim to navigate this ethical dilemma by providing a framework for vulnerability disclosure that balances the interests of users, developers, and ethical hackers. This typically involves notifying the responsible party privately, allowing sufficient time for a patch to be developed, and coordinating a public disclosure to raise awareness while minimizing harm.

Conclusion

The field of cybersecurity is not only about protecting data and systems; it also involves navigating complex ethical dilemmas. Striking the right balance between security and privacy, addressing the ethical challenges of AI, deciding on hacking back practices, ensuring cybersecurity for all, and grappling with the dilemmas of ethical hacking and responsible disclosure are crucial steps towards a more secure and ethical digital future.

As Gen-Z enters the world of cybersecurity, it is essential for them to engage in thoughtful discussions and debates surrounding these ethical dilemmas. By considering the potential consequences and weighing competing values, they can contribute to the development of ethical frameworks and practices that shape the future of cybersecurity. Remember, cybersecurity is not just about protecting your own shit; it's about building a safer and more equitable digital landscape for everyone.

Resources: - Casebooks on Cybersecurity Ethics: Engaging Students in Real-World Ethical Dilemmas by Marie Murphy and Casey Fiesler - "Ethics of Artificial Intelligence and Robotics" by Vincent C. Müller - "The Age of Surveillance Capitalism: The Fight for a Human Future at the New Frontier of Power" by Shoshana Zuboff

Index

-gritty, 60, 74

ability, 30, 123, 166
abuse, 105
abyss, 18, 20
access, 1, 3, 4, 10, 16, 18, 22, 24, 28, 37, 44, 64, 67, 71, 73, 78–81, 84, 89, 92, 94, 97, 98, 102, 105, 110, 111, 121–123, 126, 127, 131, 134, 141, 142, 159, 167
accessibility, 129, 130
account, 10, 57, 67, 76, 77, 87, 92, 94, 96, 98, 136
accountability, 6, 54, 105, 107, 108, 115, 161, 169
accountable, 20, 39, 98, 99, 105, 134, 136, 137, 148, 149
accuracy, 50
accusation, 113
act, 86, 96, 115
action, 7, 23, 40, 69, 75, 87, 93, 102, 140
activism, 27
activity, 7, 85, 94
actor, 145
addition, 64, 162

address, 12, 25, 36, 79, 85, 98, 102, 106, 108, 110, 115, 127, 157
adherence, 36
Adi Shamir, 119
adrenaline, 28, 140
advance, 25, 162
advancement, 106
advantage, 1, 7, 15, 16, 24, 36, 73, 167
advent, 168
adventure, 160
adversary, 167
advertising, 36, 97, 100
advice, 36, 137
age, 3, 6, 8, 11, 23, 36, 39, 43, 50, 53, 60, 73, 90, 98, 99, 101, 105, 109, 121, 124
agency, 142
agenda, 15
aim, 15, 33, 67, 84, 98, 105, 106, 108, 141, 170
alert, 3, 96, 152
algorithm, 118–121, 166
Alice, 119
ally, 165
alphabet, 119
alternative, 59, 100

173

amount, 53, 91, 97, 166
amusement, 54
analysis, 53, 119, 120, 143, 147, 149
analyst, 89, 143, 145, 146
Ancient Egypt, 121
angel, 150
anonymity, 20, 54, 115
answer, 84
antivirus, 9, 11, 71, 162
anxiety, 5
app, 71, 73, 92, 110, 123
applicability, 17
application, 24, 32, 34, 85, 111, 141, 156, 164
approach, 9, 14, 16, 17, 21, 51, 59, 117, 151, 161, 162, 164, 167
architecture, 83
area, 25, 27
argument, 53
arm, 3, 46, 73, 95, 103
armor, 141
array, 19
arsenal, 63, 69, 147
art, 56, 60, 142, 143, 156
artist, 142
aspect, 6, 45, 52, 124, 137, 150, 161
ass, 7, 10, 12, 57, 60, 68, 141
asset, 97, 106
attack, 4, 5, 9, 14, 15, 17, 19, 22, 24–26, 29, 45, 46, 48, 49, 67, 68, 85, 89, 94, 116, 133, 141, 143, 145, 149, 152, 168, 169
attacker, 80
attempt, 87, 88
attention, 2, 9, 23, 71, 90, 146
attorney, 142
attribution, 16, 18, 145

audits, 135
authentication, 9, 10, 44, 59, 67, 71, 73, 92, 93, 99, 133
authenticator, 92
authenticity, 89
avenue, 167, 168
awareness, 10, 11, 17, 23, 27, 52, 89, 145, 170
awesomeness, 62

back, 7, 46, 67, 72, 114, 122, 124, 132, 149, 155, 170, 171
backbone, 38, 162
background, 29
backup, 45, 72, 132
badge, 132
bag, 56
bait, 87, 90
balance, 51, 67, 93, 164, 169, 171
bank, 4, 76, 77, 84–86, 94, 97, 136, 141, 142
banking, 7, 89, 141, 154
bankruptcy, 4
barrier, 79
basis, 166
battery, 59
battle, 8, 23, 26, 126, 139, 149, 151, 160, 165
battlefield, 24
battleground, 20
bay, 47, 81
beauty, 122
beginning, 3
behalf, 110
behavior, 17, 20, 27, 36, 37, 39, 54–56, 97, 102, 115, 118, 162
being, 3, 23, 32, 37, 39, 40, 45, 47–51, 53, 54, 73, 85, 86,

Index

93, 95–97, 99, 101, 105, 112, 114–116, 118, 140–142, 149, 151, 155, 165
belief, 30
benefit, 15, 71
bias, 50
big, 11, 102, 105, 107, 108, 151
binary, 166
binge, 6
biometric, 44, 71
birth, 85, 110
bit, 43
blackmail, 38, 97, 100
block, 55, 80, 100
Bob, 119
Bob, 119
body, 55
bomb, 102
book, 53
boss, 8, 60
botnet, 155
bounty, 26, 156–158, 160
brainer, 11
breach, 16, 22, 37, 38, 102, 111, 120, 132, 134–136, 149
break, 6, 65, 112, 141, 166
breed, 13
breeding, 20, 22, 54
browsing, 36, 74, 76, 77, 99
Bruce Schneier, 8, 121
bubble, 64
buck, 15
bug, 26, 155–160, 162
building, 17, 23, 112, 133, 148, 155, 160, 171
bullet, 9
burden, 4
business, 9, 13, 18, 130, 134, 152

buy, 22, 150
bypass, 9, 67, 123, 142

call, 85, 94, 96
camaraderie, 155
Canada, 154
capture, 10, 89
card, 1, 4, 7, 9, 13, 19, 37, 85, 87, 102
care, 7, 50, 100
career, 7, 28, 149
cart, 18
case, 9, 29, 32, 72, 133, 136, 145, 146, 148, 149, 165
Casey Fiesler, 171
cash, 7, 151, 156
cat, 3, 18, 22, 24, 145
category, 27
caution, 73, 76
censorship, 20
century, 119, 168
chain, 6, 22
challenge, 17, 18, 20, 24, 26, 53, 76, 151
chamber, 141
change, 78, 110
channel, 85, 96
chaos, 5, 15, 20, 30
chapter, 26
character, 85
charge, 99
charm, 142
check, 7, 54, 56, 69, 76, 79, 83, 85, 86, 92
checking, 58
choice, 69, 149, 152
cipher, 119, 120
ciphertext, 120–122, 124
citizen, 39, 53–56, 67, 105, 112, 114

citizenship, 54, 55
city, 5
class, 83
click, 12, 87, 89, 94
clicking, 7, 12, 22, 44, 46, 92, 118
client, 151
clock, 25
cloud, 45, 52, 121, 124, 125, 127–130, 132–137
code, 10, 16, 27, 30, 92, 98, 140, 155, 156, 162, 167
coercion, 15
coffee, 10
coin, 68
coincidence, 102
collaboration, 17, 18, 25, 157, 160–162
colleague, 84
collection, 37, 99, 100, 102, 112
college, 7
combination, 40, 98, 146, 156
comfort, 110
comic, 59
command, 145, 155
comment, 6, 7, 91, 112, 113
commerce, 7
commitment, 30, 133, 161
commodity, 37, 99
communication, 5, 54–56, 98, 122–125, 166–168
community, 25, 29, 54, 145, 151, 152, 154, 155, 160, 161, 170
company, 32, 37, 89, 94, 95, 149
compartment, 132
compatibility, 168
competition, 159
complexity, 10, 21, 29, 58, 167, 168
compliance, 107, 137

component, 23, 148
compromise, 10, 16, 18, 24, 81, 110
computer, 12, 13, 24, 27, 140, 150, 166, 169, 170
computing, 25, 119, 127–130, 134, 166, 168
con, 142
concept, 59, 109, 118–121, 162, 170
concern, 23, 25
conclusion, 100
conduct, 135, 152, 162
confidence, 36, 41, 45, 124
confidentiality, 157, 167
conflict, 54
conscience, 7
consensus, 17
consent, 37, 40, 97, 98, 106, 108, 114
consideration, 169
consistency, 50
consultant, 149–152
consulting, 152
consumer, 37
contact, 90, 110
content, 110, 112–114, 122, 137
context, 26, 55, 56
continue, 67, 69, 165, 168
contractor, 152
contrast, 30
control, 8, 39, 41, 73, 81, 83, 90, 99, 101, 106, 108, 110, 112, 121, 123, 145, 155
controversy, 123
convenience, 67, 81, 127, 130, 134
conversation, 96
cooperation, 17, 18, 155, 160
corner, 11, 20, 33, 105
corporation, 141
corruption, 20

Index

cost, 81, 129
country, 16, 33, 38, 98
couple, 69, 89, 159
court, 146
cowboy, 75, 77, 131, 133
craze, 85
creation, 29, 59
creativity, 156
credential, 67–69
credibility, 50, 54
credit, 1, 4, 7, 9, 13, 19, 37, 85, 87, 102
crime, 18, 20, 56, 141, 143, 146
criminal, 1, 15, 16, 123, 142
cryptography, 25, 166–168
culture, 23, 53, 115
curiosity, 12, 22, 24, 51, 84, 87, 94
currency, 102
curve, 25
custom, 110
customer, 5, 9, 85, 86
cyber, 1–15, 17–19, 21, 23, 27, 33, 35, 36, 43–45, 67, 69, 70, 73, 81, 84, 91, 130, 133, 134, 137, 139, 143, 145, 146, 149, 151, 152, 154, 156, 160, 162–165, 169, 170
cyberbullying, 54, 90
cybercrime, 13–15, 21–23, 84, 143, 144, 146, 148, 149, 152, 155, 156, 160, 163, 165
cybercriminal, 68
cybersecurity, 4, 6–12, 15, 17–29, 33–36, 44–46, 49, 61, 63, 67, 87, 89, 94, 105, 118, 120, 121, 124, 133, 137, 139, 143–146, 149–152, 154, 155, 160–162, 165, 166, 168–171
cyberspace, 17, 18, 49, 63, 149, 164

d, 11
damage, 4–6, 24, 38, 95, 134, 135, 170
Daniel J. Levitin, 53
Daniel Kahneman, 53
darkness, 5
data, 6, 7, 9, 11, 15, 16, 22, 24, 25, 28, 33, 36–39, 41, 45, 48, 60, 64, 71–73, 80, 81, 94, 97–108, 111, 118–137, 146, 147, 149, 157, 167, 169, 171
database, 37, 141
date, 12, 22, 44, 71, 79, 80, 84, 85, 98, 99, 110, 133, 151, 162
dating, 6
day, 4, 9, 13, 16, 18, 24, 73, 90, 139, 141, 143, 146, 149
deal, 4, 6, 151
dealer, 19
debate, 17, 29, 123
decency, 53
deception, 43, 94
decision, 53, 83, 169, 170
decryption, 119, 121
dedication, 142
default, 78, 81, 84, 123
defender, 67
defense, 6, 8, 9, 11, 25, 60, 64, 67, 81, 103, 131, 137, 141, 142, 149, 160, 162–165, 170
delivery, 154
demand, 6, 23, 39, 50, 151, 152
democracy, 100

denial, 28
depression, 5
desert, 3, 133
design, 83, 167
desire, 12, 27, 84, 149, 156
destabilization, 16
detachment, 54
detail, 90, 146, 160
detection, 9, 17, 67, 89, 147, 150, 163
detective, 19, 85, 143
determination, 139
devastation, 102
development, 17, 18, 24, 119, 162, 171
device, 10, 70–72, 80, 122
dialogue, 17
Diceware, 63
dictionary, 56
difference, 7, 27, 151
difficulty, 119
dilemma, 170
diligence, 135
dirt, 7
disclosure, 5, 30, 157, 158, 170, 171
display, 94
disposal, 10, 147
disruption, 6
dissemination, 29
distance, 168
distinction, 29
distress, 102
distribution, 168, 170
disturbance, 167
dive, 18, 43, 45, 46, 53, 56, 57, 60, 67, 70, 74, 77, 87, 90, 102, 118, 121, 127, 130, 139, 141–143, 155, 165
diversity, 54

document, 115, 142
documentary, 8
domain, 67, 94, 141, 165
dominance, 16
doom, 7
door, 56, 131
dose, 7
doubt, 55, 93
downfall, 5
download, 22
Doxing, 40, 115, 116
doxing, 40, 90, 115–117
drawbridge, 132
dream, 112
drive, 45, 152
driver, 15
drug, 19
dumbass, 45–49

e, 7
ease, 81
eavesdropping, 167
echo, 52
economy, 6
ecosystem, 19, 36, 37, 81, 155, 156
edge, 15, 16
education, 18
effect, 167
effectiveness, 26, 126, 135
effort, 10, 12, 23, 60, 113, 154, 160, 170
election, 17
electricity, 16
element, 22
elephant, 90
email, 12, 40, 46, 76, 89, 94, 118, 123, 125
Emotet, 154
empathy, 54, 56, 84, 115

employee, 89
employment, 4
encryption, 22, 25, 61, 99, 118–127, 130, 132, 133, 135, 149, 150, 166–168
end, 21, 98, 120–124
endeavor, 155
endpoint, 17
enemy, 21, 141
enforcement, 13, 19, 20, 22, 106, 123, 142, 146, 154
engagement, 17
engineer, 85
engineering, 9, 22, 24, 43, 46, 47, 84, 86, 87, 92–94, 141, 142, 151
entity, 84
entry, 79, 132
environment, 54, 55, 108, 115, 151, 156, 157, 163, 166
equivalent, 18, 132
era, 119, 166, 167
erosion, 169
error, 167
espionage, 1, 13, 15, 21, 134
essay, 53
event, 132, 135
evidence, 50–52, 135, 143, 146, 148, 149
evil, 9, 126
evolution, 118, 120
example, 9, 10, 14, 17, 20, 29, 36, 59, 75, 94, 95, 100, 110, 119, 120, 136, 141, 142, 152, 154, 169, 170
exchange, 81, 155, 156, 160, 168
executive, 89, 95
exercise, 39, 73, 76
experience, 66, 81, 93

expertise, 25, 27, 146, 148, 149, 151, 155, 156, 160, 165, 170
exploit, 1, 8, 9, 12, 13, 18, 22–27, 30, 36, 44, 68, 80, 81, 90, 94, 98, 118, 134, 141, 151, 156, 170
exploitation, 161
exploiting, 56, 83, 84, 140, 142
exposure, 120
extent, 100, 149
extortion, 97, 134
extremist, 20
eye, 160

fabric, 167
face, 4, 5, 13, 22, 24, 32, 35, 41, 50, 55, 56, 70, 87, 90, 96, 100, 149–151, 159, 167, 168, 170
fact, 10, 54, 56, 68, 122
factor, 9, 10, 59, 64, 92, 93, 99, 133, 166
faint, 145
fairness, 170
fake, 9, 89
fallout, 4, 38, 102
fame, 155
family, 8, 12, 40
fan, 103
fear, 11, 20, 21, 46, 57, 73, 87, 141, 161
feat, 23, 166
feature, 79, 80, 110, 111
feed, 55
field, 7, 25, 26, 28, 49, 67, 146, 149, 151, 155, 162, 166, 168, 169, 171
fight, 14, 20, 146, 148, 152, 156, 163
file, 147

finding, 12, 85, 93, 151, 152, 156, 159, 161
fine, 27–29
fingerprint, 10
finish, 122
fire, 20, 132
firewall, 79
firm, 152
firmware, 79, 80
fish, 11, 89
fishing, 87
fitness, 81
fix, 10, 27, 30, 98, 142, 157
flaw, 111
focus, 54, 55, 57, 79, 137, 162
fog, 127, 129
fool, 49, 96
footprint, 5, 6, 44, 91, 99, 102, 109, 111, 112, 115
force, 10, 56, 64
foreclosure, 4
forensic, 143, 149
forgiveness, 29
form, 10, 25, 38, 85, 87, 92, 94, 106, 124, 166, 170
format, 121, 132, 135, 157
fortification, 125
fortress, 11, 23, 57, 59, 67, 77, 105, 127
foster, 18, 155, 161, 162
foundation, 106, 125, 150, 166, 167
framework, 33, 158, 167, 170
fraud, 13, 38, 95–97, 100, 134, 146
freedom, 20, 30
frequency, 33, 119, 120
friend, 6, 11, 12, 57, 63, 85, 110
front, 56, 131, 160, 162
frontier, 21, 73, 105, 142
fun, 59, 85, 89, 90

functionality, 81
fundamental, 30, 41, 118, 161, 166
future, 6–8, 29, 107, 145, 165, 166, 168, 171

gain, 1, 4, 5, 13, 15, 16, 22, 24, 27, 28, 36, 37, 44, 64, 67, 78, 80, 81, 84, 87, 89, 94, 97, 102, 134, 141, 142, 157, 160, 162, 167
game, 6, 11, 22, 24, 49, 67, 89, 100, 141, 145
gaming, 77
gang, 132
gap, 170
gateway, 73, 77
gathering, 1, 15, 85, 115, 141, 143
gazillion, 60
Gen-Z, 12
geotagging, 110
glimmer, 20
glimpse, 3, 20, 21
globe, 20
gloom, 7
go, 11, 18, 62, 63, 67, 77
goal, 12, 27, 46, 51, 54, 58, 67, 89, 146, 156, 161
gold, 6, 68
goldmine, 4, 44, 97
good, 7, 10, 27, 30, 44, 64, 65, 67, 110, 114, 126, 141, 155
goodwill, 94
gossip, 114
government, 14, 17, 20, 50, 97, 109, 145
grade, 61
grasp, 65, 102, 150, 166
grid, 5, 15
ground, 20, 22, 54, 92

group, 145, 149
guard, 118
guardian, 150
guest, 80
guide, 30, 106, 139
gunslinger, 69, 73, 105, 140, 141, 149

habit, 72, 79
hack, 15, 149
hacker, 7, 9, 10, 19, 24, 29, 32, 64, 122, 139, 140, 142
hacking, 10, 11, 13, 19, 21, 22, 24, 26–32, 139–142, 145, 156, 160, 162, 170, 171
hacktivist, 5
halt, 5
hand, 27, 28, 121, 142, 166
handing, 7
handling, 99, 108
handshake, 64
Hans Rosling et al, 53
harassment, 40, 90
hardness, 166, 167
hardware, 16
harm, 27, 30, 32, 40, 96–98, 110, 114, 116, 118, 143, 170
harmonization, 108
Harry Potter, 85
hash, 167
hat, 26–30, 130, 141, 170
hate, 20
haven, 22
havoc, 1, 4, 6, 19, 94, 103, 115, 133, 143, 146
head, 19, 166
headache, 19
health, 53, 93
heart, 145

hell, 8, 57, 64
help, 27, 28, 44, 53, 54, 79, 86, 87, 89, 106, 111, 114, 125, 142, 147, 156, 161
hero, 11, 29, 142
highlight, 107, 159
history, 3, 4, 36, 97
hold, 54, 99, 102, 105, 121, 122, 134, 137, 146
hole, 16
home, 40, 77–81, 83, 110, 115
hope, 8, 10, 11, 20
horde, 21
horizon, 2
horse, 59
host, 23
hotspot, 77
house, 131
hub, 19, 158
human, 9, 13, 20, 22, 84, 94, 142, 151, 165
hunt, 143, 155
hunter, 157
hunting, 92, 156, 158–160
hurricane, 56
hygiene, 10, 45

idea, 167
identification, 37, 64, 87, 94, 149
identity, 1, 4, 6, 13, 37, 43, 78, 86, 90, 94, 97, 100, 102, 112, 113, 115, 116, 134
ideology, 24
image, 92, 112
imbalance, 170
impact, 4, 6, 8, 14, 26, 28, 30, 32, 37, 38, 53, 89, 105, 107, 108, 112, 120, 134, 135, 141, 150, 152, 159, 162, 163

impersonation, 85, 94–96, 142, 151
implement, 17, 65, 130, 150
implementation, 106
importance, 6–8, 10, 27, 45, 53, 56, 59, 60, 93, 97, 105, 111, 112, 130, 136, 155, 157, 160
impunity, 22
in, 1–32, 35–39, 41, 43–46, 48–50, 53–61, 63, 64, 67–76, 78–81, 83–85, 87, 89, 90, 92–94, 96–100, 102, 104, 106–108, 110–112, 114, 115, 118–128, 132–137, 141–152, 154–171
inability, 122
incident, 17, 36, 111, 135, 150, 162
inclination, 94
inclusion, 123
increase, 7
indictment, 149
individual, 5, 9, 15, 16, 23, 32, 94, 115, 160
industry, 150, 155, 160, 162, 170
influence, 53, 101, 108
information, 1, 4–7, 9–13, 15, 16, 19, 20, 22, 23, 25, 26, 30, 36, 37, 40, 44, 46, 50, 51, 54, 60, 70, 72, 73, 76, 77, 84–87, 89–94, 96–102, 105, 106, 109–112, 114–116, 118–121, 124, 126, 130, 134, 136, 141–143, 146, 151–155, 157, 160, 161, 166, 168
infrastructure, 1, 5, 6, 15, 16, 33, 36, 136, 141, 145, 150, 154, 156, 168
injection, 141

innocence, 4
innovation, 18
input, 76
insider, 134
instance, 10, 15, 22, 162
instant, 4, 87, 94, 151
institution, 141
integrity, 80, 119, 158, 162, 167
intel, 85
intelligence, 1, 15–17, 19, 21, 137, 161
intent, 13, 27, 28, 30, 32
intention, 30
interception, 98
interest, 97, 162
interference, 17, 166
internet, 8, 15, 18, 20, 41, 43, 54, 73, 77, 79–81, 113, 115, 122
interview, 112
introduction, 123
intruder, 167
intrusion, 17, 150
invasion, 100, 102
investigation, 145, 149
investigator, 143
involvement, 29
isogeny, 167
isolation, 21
issue, 16

job, 7, 112, 150, 152, 160
Johannes Buchmann, 121
joke, 6
journey, 3, 29, 69, 105
judgment, 52
Julius Caesar, 118, 119
jurisdiction, 141
justice, 146, 149, 170

Index

Kanye, 130
Kevin Mitnick, 8
key, 4, 17, 20, 27, 33, 38, 43, 53, 85, 86, 90, 98, 106–108, 119–122, 124, 141, 150, 158, 163, 167, 168
keyword, 119
kick, 10, 12
kickass, 69
kill, 29
kind, 48
kindness, 54
kingdom, 60, 63
kitten, 18
know, 6, 7, 12, 18, 20, 57, 58, 60, 74, 78, 85, 88, 94, 95, 102, 110, 130, 140, 167
knowledge, 3, 7, 8, 11, 12, 15, 21, 23, 25, 27, 30, 46, 63, 69, 73, 76, 77, 89, 95–97, 103, 105, 106, 120, 139, 141, 142, 145, 149, 151, 152, 155, 160, 162

lack, 17, 55, 81, 100, 170
landscape, 1, 7, 10, 11, 13, 15, 19, 21, 23, 29, 36, 41, 49, 102, 107, 108, 111, 112, 123, 125, 133, 145, 163, 165, 166, 168, 169, 171
language, 55, 112
lasso, 131
lattice, 167
law, 13, 19, 20, 28–30, 141, 142, 146
layer, 10, 21, 64, 66, 67, 79, 92, 135
learning, 3, 8, 56, 141, 155
legitimacy, 44
length, 58
Leonard Adleman, 119

letter, 119
level, 43, 49, 67, 89, 96, 110, 121, 142, 162
life, 4–8, 43, 44, 54, 60, 61, 73, 75, 85, 89, 102, 109, 110, 118, 140, 141
light, 20, 68, 149
lightning, 11, 166
likelihood, 17
limit, 91, 98, 114
limitation, 108
line, 26–31, 60, 131, 149, 150
link, 6, 7, 22, 76, 87, 89, 93, 94
lion, 18
list, 53, 110
location, 91, 99, 110, 111
lock, 12, 121, 124, 130
locking, 131
logarithm, 166
login, 10, 76, 78, 89, 94
look, 2, 8, 34, 89, 104, 107, 119, 123, 143, 145, 149
loss, 4, 5, 72, 78, 102, 122, 134
lot, 91
love, 18, 152
lowercase, 98
loyalty, 5

machine, 1, 73
mafia, 13
making, 9, 13, 16, 19, 20, 26, 49, 53, 81, 119, 124, 131, 132, 135, 167, 169
malware, 1, 9, 18, 22, 24, 29, 48, 77, 83, 145, 147, 149, 154
man, 49
management, 57, 60, 79, 122
manager, 10, 44, 62, 63, 100, 112
managing, 73, 109, 111, 112, 151

manipulation, 84, 151
manner, 10, 67, 106
manufacturer, 79
Marcus, 29
Marcus Hutchins, 29
Marie Murphy, 171
market, 7
marketing, 102
marketplace, 19
master, 142
mathematician, 166
Matt Bishop, 8
matter, 57, 60
mattress, 133
mayhem, 102
maze, 33, 35, 36
mean, 50, 57, 85, 101
means, 7, 9, 15, 30, 37, 54, 84, 112, 120, 122, 166
measure, 122
measurement, 167
media, 6, 11, 36, 37, 44, 50, 52, 53, 77, 85, 87, 89–93, 97–100, 109–112, 114, 116, 155
menace, 68
mess, 104
message, 16, 93, 119, 121, 122
messaging, 98, 111, 120–123, 125
metadata, 122
method, 59, 63, 121, 168
methodology, 140
middle, 49
midst, 123
military, 15, 61, 119
million, 111, 136
mind, 37, 51, 73, 84, 92, 125, 166
mindful, 44, 50, 52, 55, 92, 93, 99–101, 109, 112, 115, 118

mindset, 24, 26, 29, 96, 105, 139
minefield, 112
misconception, 9
misinformation, 54, 100
mission, 141, 152
mistake, 54, 78
misuse, 98, 105
model, 75
moment, 55, 56, 64, 65, 74, 76, 130
money, 4, 7, 19, 96, 151
monitoring, 24, 79, 102, 136, 147
morning, 4, 77
motion, 83
motivation, 116
mouse, 22, 24, 145
move, 45, 70, 77, 81, 99, 102, 121, 124, 141
multivariate, 167

name, 4, 7, 36, 85, 94, 102, 112
narrative, 50
nation, 15–18, 21, 149
nature, 18, 21–23, 43, 45, 94, 116
need, 3, 4, 6, 9–11, 22, 23, 30, 33, 60, 64, 78, 90, 93, 100, 107–109, 114, 115, 121, 122, 130, 132, 133, 136, 139–141, 143, 146, 150, 151, 157, 158, 160, 166
negative, 110, 113
neighborhood, 18, 56, 152
net, 8, 87, 89, 133
network, 10, 17, 19, 24, 77–81, 83, 141, 145, 147, 149, 155, 156, 160–163
networking, 150
news, 11, 44, 50
night, 130
nightmare, 5, 102

ninja, 63
nitty, 60, 67, 74
noise, 168
non, 107
norm, 55
North Korea, 15, 149
note, 31
nuisance, 12
number, 67, 85, 86, 94, 96, 98, 102, 116, 119

obfuscation, 16
objective, 1
observer, 167
offer, 25, 58, 80, 100, 135, 158, 160–162
official, 86, 89
one, 4, 8, 10, 15, 18, 19, 24–26, 54, 62, 68, 71, 77, 80, 84, 86, 87, 90, 94, 98, 116, 123, 133, 139, 141, 142, 145, 150–152, 154, 160, 161, 166
online, 5–7, 10–12, 20, 27, 36–40, 43–45, 53–56, 58–60, 75–78, 81, 84, 87, 89, 90, 92–94, 97–102, 109, 110, 112–115, 117, 118, 121, 141, 155, 167, 169
operating, 9, 21–23, 140
operation, 143
opinion, 52
opportunity, 133, 151, 155
option, 12, 80, 127
order, 12
organization, 5, 9, 23, 26, 94, 142, 152, 156, 157, 161, 162
other, 9–11, 16, 19, 20, 22, 24, 27, 28, 43, 44, 54, 68, 72, 77, 80, 81, 84, 90, 121, 146, 149, 150, 166
out, 4, 6–8, 15, 18, 19, 28, 46, 52, 55, 56, 58, 67–69, 76–78, 83, 85, 86, 89, 92, 101, 112, 116, 159
outlaw, 132
oversharing, 6, 85, 90, 93
owner, 9, 27, 30

pace, 23
padlock, 121
page, 89
paid, 149, 152
pain, 60, 68
pair, 102, 119, 121
paper, 56
par, 58
paradise, 19
paranoia, 43–45
part, 7, 9, 10, 26, 30, 37, 54, 90, 109, 126, 127, 134, 150
partner, 67, 77, 133, 139, 146, 152, 163
party, 110, 170
passcode, 71
passion, 156, 160
passphrase, 59, 124
password, 10, 12, 44, 56–64, 67–69, 78, 80, 87, 92, 98, 100, 131
past, 1, 29, 112
patch, 24, 156, 170
patching, 17
path, 29, 149
pattern, 119
pay, 71, 90, 151
penetration, 140, 141
people, 7, 9–12, 20, 54, 68, 85, 87, 92, 110, 142, 149, 151, 152

performance, 79
performer, 133
permission, 30
perpetrator, 143
persistence, 156
person, 160
perspective, 8
persuasion, 142
Peter Shor, 166
phase, 140
phisher, 89
phishing, 4, 7, 12, 22, 43, 46, 63, 87–90, 94, 142, 151, 152
phone, 40, 85, 92, 94, 96, 98, 111, 116
photo, 7, 112
physics, 166, 168
pick, 19
pickpocket, 12
picture, 85
piece, 102, 146
place, 9, 18, 19, 27, 59, 60, 77, 98, 117, 155, 156
plaintext, 120, 124
plan, 135, 140
planning, 17
platform, 20, 68, 89, 90, 110, 111, 154, 160
playground, 90, 124
playing, 67
plenty, 7, 21
plethora, 144
point, 75, 79, 145
pond, 11
popularity, 50, 123, 127, 156, 161
porn, 5
pornography, 20
portal, 89
position, 15

positive, 28, 39, 54, 56, 112, 113, 115, 152
positivity, 55
possibility, 116
post, 6, 7, 53, 54, 85, 90, 91, 109, 110, 112, 113, 167, 168
posture, 157, 161, 162
potential, 7, 11, 12, 22, 24–26, 31, 32, 38, 43–45, 70, 77, 79, 91–93, 97, 98, 103, 111, 118, 120, 127, 129, 130, 134, 135, 137, 150, 152, 162–166, 169–171
power, 5, 7, 11, 14, 15, 30, 44, 54, 56, 63, 93, 119, 127, 132, 151, 154, 160, 166, 167
practice, 40, 64, 89, 170
precaution, 133
predictability, 58
presence, 44, 112, 115, 118, 167
pressure, 15, 96, 169
prevention, 163
prey, 22, 46, 76, 96, 141, 151
price, 75
principle, 30
privacy, 6, 23, 36–39, 41, 44, 71, 73, 81, 90, 91, 93, 98–102, 105–112, 114, 119, 121–124, 126, 129, 134, 150, 161, 169, 171
problem, 19, 150
process, 11, 98, 111, 113, 115, 120, 121, 124, 145, 151, 157, 166
processing, 166
product, 53
profession, 140, 141
professional, 5, 39, 110, 112, 162
profile, 8, 17, 26, 85, 149

Index

profit, 36, 105
program, 26, 152, 157
programming, 140, 150, 156
project, 92
proliferation, 17
promise, 25
property, 13–15, 134, 166
prosecution, 142
protection, 17, 36, 66, 67, 79, 81, 92, 99, 135, 151, 160
provider, 84, 132, 135
prowess, 142
prowl, 4
psychology, 22, 142, 151
public, 6, 9, 11, 72, 73, 91, 112, 119, 121, 157, 170
purchase, 78, 97
purpose, 30, 108
puzzle, 85, 143, 146

quantum, 25, 120, 166–168
quest, 15, 159
question, 44, 46, 50, 54, 90
quiz, 85
qwerty, 57

race, 20, 22–26, 167, 168
radar, 67
range, 1, 24, 27, 102, 116, 134, 150, 156, 162, 167
ransom, 1, 102
ransomware, 1, 4, 14, 29, 43, 48, 145, 154
reach, 13, 23, 86
read, 43, 110, 111, 120, 121, 123, 124
reader, 64, 102, 105
reality, 4, 5, 7, 78, 100, 105, 168

realm, 6, 7, 18, 21, 27, 102, 121, 139, 156, 166
reason, 79
reasoning, 83
recipient, 87, 120–123
recognition, 84, 107, 156, 157, 160
reconnaissance, 140, 141
recovery, 147
redemption, 29
reference, 50
reflection, 8, 113
refrain, 54
reinforcement, 152
relationship, 161
reminder, 111
report, 25, 30, 55, 142, 156, 157, 160, 161
reporting, 140, 155, 157
representation, 97
representative, 85
reprisal, 20
reputation, 5–7, 32, 39, 95, 102, 110, 112–115, 135
request, 71, 86, 87
research, 17, 18, 26, 53, 135, 168
resilience, 17
resort, 115
respect, 53, 54, 56, 114
response, 17, 22, 36, 135, 150, 162, 163
responsibility, 11, 23, 31, 36, 44, 54, 56, 134–136
rest, 59, 80, 135
result, 4, 22, 23, 55, 81, 122, 169
return, 156
revelation, 29
revenue, 5, 97
review, 98, 110, 111
revolver, 141

reward, 156
ride, 21, 26, 130, 139, 140, 149, 152
right, 6, 7, 11, 28, 29, 41, 62, 70, 77, 78, 96, 114, 132, 164, 169, 171
rise, 7, 14, 15, 21, 26, 37, 53, 97
risk, 5, 11, 17, 23, 40, 71, 91, 103, 117, 122, 135, 150
roadmap, 139
rodeo, 133
role, 5, 7, 11, 20, 23, 25, 29, 35, 89, 98, 107, 108, 118, 124, 127, 134, 143, 146, 148–150, 159, 160, 165, 170
Ron Rivest, 119
rookie, 78
room, 90
router, 78, 79
rule, 60, 85

sabotage, 15
safety, 6, 43–45, 76, 90, 118, 133
sale, 19
sand, 112
sanity, 57
sarcasm, 55
saving, 5
scalability, 129
scale, 145
scam, 7, 89
scammer, 85
scan, 8, 10
scanning, 80, 141
scenario, 5, 32, 95, 112, 120
scene, 143
science, 150, 156
scripting, 141
scrutiny, 51

search, 3, 18, 100, 161
second, 10, 64, 92
secret, 16, 64, 119, 124, 132
section, 1, 4, 8, 10, 18, 21, 24, 43, 45, 46, 49, 53, 56, 59, 60, 67, 70, 73, 76, 77, 81, 83, 87, 90, 93, 97, 105, 109, 112, 116, 118, 120, 121, 124, 126, 127, 130, 133, 134, 137, 139, 143, 149, 155, 156, 160, 166, 169
sector, 17
security, 6, 7, 10, 12, 14, 15, 17, 18, 22–25, 27, 30, 32, 36, 44, 58, 60, 64, 67, 69, 71–73, 78–81, 83, 85, 90, 92, 93, 96, 98, 99, 102, 108, 111, 119–124, 126–129, 134–136, 140–142, 150, 156–162, 167, 169–171
segmentation, 17, 80
self, 52, 113, 170
selfie, 6
sender, 118, 120, 122
sense, 31, 54, 89, 94, 132, 155
sequence, 146
series, 6
service, 10, 28, 45, 84–86, 121–123, 127, 132, 134–137
set, 9, 10, 30, 79, 90, 127, 128, 153, 170
setting, 78, 106, 132
severity, 162
shade, 27
shape, 171
share, 10, 12, 20, 36, 44, 83, 91, 93, 98, 100, 109–112, 127, 134, 142, 148, 152, 155, 160, 161

Index

sharing, 7, 9, 12, 21, 25, 54, 90, 98, 110, 111, 114, 118, 151–155, 160, 162
sharpshooter, 140
sheriff, 130, 132
Sherlock Holmeses, 146
shift, 119, 137
shit, 1, 3, 4, 6–8, 10–12, 15, 23, 26, 41, 46, 56, 60, 63, 67–69, 73, 77, 81, 84, 86, 90, 94, 96, 102, 103, 105, 109, 112, 127, 130, 133, 140, 143, 146, 149, 150, 152, 155, 171
shitstorm, 102
shooter, 149
shootout, 140
shop, 10, 19
shopping, 18, 99
Shoshana Zuboff, 171
showdown, 86
side, 18, 24, 28, 29, 68, 90, 93
signature, 9
significance, 59, 93, 166
Simon Singh, 121
site, 141
situation, 7, 76, 118, 161
size, 9
skeptical, 51, 95, 96
skepticism, 22, 43, 45, 47, 51, 93, 96
skill, 142
sleeve, 151
smartphone, 70–73, 75, 110
Snapchat, 111
snapping, 6
society, 105, 115
software, 8, 9, 11, 12, 16, 19, 24, 27, 32, 44, 48, 79–81, 98, 141, 156, 161, 162, 170

solution, 10
sophistication, 33
source, 12, 93, 94, 155
sovereignty, 17
space, 7, 54
spectrum, 28
speculation, 17
speech, 20
speed, 11, 166
spoofing, 94
spot, 7, 87, 88
spraying, 67–69
spread, 9, 29, 54, 83, 100
spyware, 48
stability, 18, 95
stage, 15
staple, 59
start, 90, 122, 124, 141, 152
starting, 145
state, 1, 5, 15–18, 21, 149, 166
status, 9, 170
staying, 14, 26, 28, 29, 36, 73, 89, 90, 93, 95, 111, 112, 114, 126, 133, 150, 151
step, 11, 18, 19, 24, 50, 67, 81, 86, 90, 97, 114, 133, 142, 150, 151, 157, 160
Steven Novella, 53
stop, 3, 19
storage, 45, 125
store, 61, 71, 98, 100, 127, 130, 134, 166
storm, 155
story, 27
strain, 17
stranger, 6
strap, 1
strategy, 9, 11, 19, 23, 59
street, 155

strength, 8, 58, 59, 119
stress, 4
string, 10
stronghold, 141
stuff, 6
stuffing, 67–69
style, 59, 89
substitution, 119
success, 39, 155
suicide, 5
summary, 18
sunset, 133, 142
superhero, 7, 160
superposition, 166
supply, 5
surface, 18
surveillance, 169
survey, 6, 85
swag, 156
switch, 29
system, 27, 30, 48, 83, 102, 141, 156, 167

tactic, 24
tag, 110
tailgating, 142
tailor, 97, 100, 102
target, 6, 8, 9, 11, 15, 18, 37, 40, 44, 57, 77, 87, 89, 97, 106, 116, 169
task, 18, 33, 133, 169
team, 12, 30
tech, 6, 102, 105, 107, 108, 161
technique, 16, 87
technology, 2, 3, 7, 12, 13, 21, 23, 25, 97, 99, 106, 123, 129, 149, 150, 152, 166, 169
tension, 123, 169
territory, 96

test, 12, 52, 58, 69, 76, 89, 135, 141, 156
testing, 59, 141, 156, 158
text, 85, 87, 94, 121–123
the United States, 154
The Wild West, 160
the Wild West, 6, 15, 63, 73, 105, 149, 160
the Wild West's, 132
theft, 1, 4, 6, 13–15, 28, 37, 43, 72, 78, 90, 94, 97, 100, 102, 116, 134, 141
thing, 7, 18, 94
think, 6, 7, 11, 56, 58, 91, 102, 118, 150, 151
thinking, 50, 52–54, 57, 93, 94, 96, 146, 162, 165
thought, 19, 112
threat, 1, 10, 15, 17, 18, 25, 29, 49, 98, 117, 124, 145, 149, 155, 163
thrill, 1, 24, 155
time, 3, 6, 7, 10, 11, 13, 45, 52, 53, 58, 62, 69, 76, 79, 80, 85, 86, 90, 103, 110, 111, 119, 121, 130, 133, 135, 152, 157, 159, 160, 163, 170
timing, 122
tip, 63
to, 1, 3–33, 36–41, 43–46, 49–60, 62–74, 76–81, 83–103, 105–137, 139–152, 154–171
today, 1, 5, 8, 43, 44, 84, 102, 109, 112, 119, 124, 130
toe, 150
toll, 5
tone, 55, 56
tool, 19, 123

Index 191

top, 151
topic, 8, 53, 136
touch, 93
town, 132, 149
trace, 22
tracing, 115
track, 6, 13, 100, 110
tracking, 37
trade, 15, 19, 134
traffic, 79, 145
trafficking, 20
trail, 109
training, 17, 18, 23, 150, 162
transfer, 89, 141
transit, 135
transmission, 122
transparency, 100, 161
transportation, 5, 14, 15
trap, 47, 51, 54, 85
treasure, 19, 70, 141
triage, 162
trick, 7, 12, 43, 84, 87, 96, 142
troll, 53, 56
trolling, 53
trouble, 150
trove, 19, 70
trust, 5, 6, 8, 17, 22, 24, 44, 57, 60,
    86, 87, 92, 94, 106, 108,
    110, 114, 142, 150, 151,
    161, 162
trustworthiness, 122
truth, 8, 143, 149
tumbleweed, 141
tweet, 7
twin, 9
type, 94

Ukraine, 15
underbelly, 18

underground, 13, 19
understanding, 8, 18, 24, 26, 31, 33,
    36, 45, 55, 83, 96, 99, 101,
    120, 121, 129, 140, 142,
    150, 151, 156
universe, 6
up, 1, 4–7, 9–12, 18, 19, 21, 22, 26,
    41, 44, 49, 58, 60, 64,
    71–74, 77–80, 84, 93, 98,
    99, 102, 105, 118, 121,
    132, 133, 139–142, 146,
    150–152, 162, 163
upbringing, 52
update, 12, 76, 87, 110, 135, 141,
    145
uppercase, 98
urge, 55
urgency, 86, 87, 94, 162
US, 15, 17
use, 7–11, 13, 15, 16, 18, 20, 24, 27,
    37, 55, 72, 80, 81, 84, 89,
    94, 96, 98, 100, 102, 109,
    111, 119, 120, 124, 137,
    141, 149, 156, 166, 169
user, 67, 100, 111, 119, 123, 170
username, 68, 78

vacation, 98
validity, 54
valuable, 16, 36, 97, 99, 102, 106,
    143, 161, 162
value, 30, 37, 50, 97, 99, 102, 160
variety, 150
vault, 61
Veracrypt, 126
verification, 10, 92
verify, 12, 50, 86, 87, 93, 94, 96
version, 119

victim, 4–7, 23, 40, 45, 48, 68, 87, 96, 117, 170
victimization, 5
video, 123
view, 110
vigilance, 11, 15, 151
vigilante, 141
vigilantism, 170
Vincent C. Müller, 171
violation, 134
violence, 20
visibility, 114
voice, 20, 55, 81, 84, 123
vulnerability, 22, 32, 83, 94, 111, 141, 156, 157, 160, 162, 170

waiting, 6, 8, 43, 73
wake, 102, 104
walk, 27
warfare, 1, 15, 17, 21
watch, 46, 85, 92, 152
water, 5
watering, 16
way, 2, 67, 80, 85, 92, 107, 112–114, 119, 121, 124, 127, 155, 161
wealth, 162
weapon, 2, 148, 149
web, 10, 13, 18, 21, 22, 24, 74, 76, 100, 102, 141, 156
webpage, 76
website, 37, 75, 79, 85, 94
weight, 112
well, 1, 3, 7, 13, 16, 44, 46, 54, 93, 95, 96, 112, 114, 123, 133, 140, 143, 150, 160, 168
west, 3, 10–12, 18, 21–23, 26, 29, 41, 44, 45, 49, 67, 69, 84, 86, 87, 93, 96, 99, 120, 124, 126, 133, 143, 146, 149, 168
whole, 105, 121, 127
Wild West, 70, 73, 74, 77, 152, 160, 162, 170
wilderness, 115, 118
win, 7, 54, 161
window, 28
wire, 89
wolf, 141
work, 2, 14, 24, 27, 30, 80, 87, 115, 145, 146, 152
workforce, 18
working, 143, 150, 155
workplace, 86
world, 1, 2, 5, 7, 8, 11, 12, 15, 18, 20, 21, 23, 27–30, 33, 39, 43–46, 48, 49, 53, 54, 56, 67, 77, 79, 81, 82, 84, 87, 89, 90, 93, 94, 97, 99, 100, 102, 105, 110, 112, 116–121, 124, 130, 139, 141–144, 146, 149, 151, 152, 154–156, 159, 160, 165–169, 171
worry, 81
worth, 6, 7, 60, 100, 111, 160
writing, 89
wrong, 40, 60, 73, 85, 98, 100

Milton Keynes UK
Ingram Content Group UK Ltd.
UKHW030743121124
451094UK00013B/1012